D1066360

a_website_that_works
/how_marketing_
agencies_can
_create_business_
generating_sites

/mark_o'brien

a_website_that_works

/how_marketing_
agencies_can
_create_business_
generating_sites

/mark_o'brien

rockbench
PUBLISHING

RockBench Publishing Corp.
6101 Stillmeadow Dr.,
Nashville, TN 37211
www.rockbench.com

Interior design by Faceout Studio
Interior illustrations by Chris Butler and Justin Kerr

Library of Congress Control Number: 2011930327

Printed in the United States of America
First edition, 2011

ISBN-13: 978-1-60544-008-8

rockbench
PUBLISHING

courageous thought leadership content

/introduction/

This book offers a guide for creating websites, for both your firm and your clients, that have a significant and measurable impact on revenues. While outlining a reliable planning process you can use to consistently build business-generating sites, it also demystifies the aspects of web development that keep many firms from completing sites on strategy, on time, and on budget.

You know you have to market your firm. You also know that the best opportunity you have to consistently reach and engage new prospects is through your website. As a professional marketer, it is now your business to have a mastery of this dominant marketing medium. Your clients and prospects are asking you increasingly educated questions about website marketing, and the business is often won or lost by your answers.

Your site can be yet another brochure for your business, or it can be the sole source of twenty percent of your closed new business each year. What better way to develop your web expertise than by creating a site for your firm that brings in new business while proving your web marketing capabilities? Your prospects will be living case studies of your web expertise each time they find and contact you through your site.

My company, Newfangled, has worked closely with marketing firms for over fifteen years. As a result, we have had the unique opportunity to observe which on-site marketing tactics work for them and which do not. Throughout this book, I will focus on your website. However, these principles can be successfully applied to any conversion-focused marketing website. I encourage you to use the process outlined in this book on your own site first, in order to understand and to personalize it, and then apply it to every client site you build in the future.

A NOTE ON WHO YOU ARE

If you work for a marketing firm and are interested in the web, this book is for you. If you own a marketing firm with roughly one hundred or fewer employees, then this book is really for you. I understand that this focus limits the total readership of this book considerably, and I have no problem with that. Yours is the situation I understand in great detail . In this book, I freely interchange the terms agency, marketing firm, and firm. In all cases, I am referring to your business. </ >

/the_9_step_process_for planning_a_ marketing_ website/

YOUR WEBSITE IS A WORK OF COMMERCE, NOT A WORK OF ART.

Why do you have a website?

This may sound like a foolish question, but it should be the first one you ask when starting every new web project, especially when building your own site. Judging from the many agency sites I see, most principals do not ask themselves this question, or, if they do, they do not seem to take the time to really think about the answer.

Many agencies believe that their site's central function is to show their visitors how creative they are. I disagree. Certainly, a portion of the site should serve this purpose, but this is not the primary purpose of the site. The site's key role is to generate business for the firm, and demonstrating creativity is only part of what converts a visitor into a

ROLES ▼	QUESTIONS ▼	ELEMENTS ▼
Attract	Who is my audience?	Personas
Inform	What do they want from me?	Content Strategy
Engage	What do I want from them?	Calls to Action

NEWFANGLED'S 9-STEP PLANNING PROCESS

prospect. Designing a website with the primary goal of demonstrating creativity is akin to an architect designing a demo house with the sole intent of showing how many different styles she can design. The result would be an interesting house but not one anyone would ever choose to live in or buy.

The same is true of your website. The site, first and foremost, needs to be a highly usable site. You will not lose a site visitor because the home page is not splashy enough, but you will lose plenty if the site is so "creative" that the visitor cannot figure out how to get to your portfolio section within the first five seconds of landing on the site, for example.

The site is the vehicle that attracts the right prospects to your company. It should intuitively guide them to the pages that interest them the most and entice them to engage with you on a more meaningful level at some point during that first visit. Your site is a tour visitors can take of your firm, but it is a self-guided tour, and visitors will probably not follow the path that you expect.

One indicator that your website is performing well is if visitors can easily learn about the various aspects of your firm as they move through your site based on their interests. The more accurately the site describes your firm's expertise across different media (imagery, text, video, etc.), and the more intuitive the navigation is between those descriptions, the more successful the site will be. Your portfolio will certainly be part of the tour visitors take, but it is not the only thing they want to know about.

When first approaching your website redesign, it is important to consider your basic strategic plan for the site before jumping into the "real" work of building the site. To help you add some structure to the strategic planning stage of your site, I created a 9 Step Process. This process is designed to help you take a more objective look at why you have a website in the first place. Taking a week or two at the beginning of the web development project to work on your site's strategy will undoubtedly have a significant and positive effect on the results the site ends up delivering for you. This practice could also extend your site's shelf-life by a number of years.

Websites take a lot of time, money, and energy to create, and you risk wasting all three of these commodities unless you have a specific plan for the goals of your site. Just winging it and hoping for the best might create a site that represents your firm well enough for the next six to eighteen months, but that approach is unlikely to create a site that has a significant impact on your business over the long term. My goal for you is to create a site that will be an effective revenue-generation tool for your business for three to five years, after which point web design and technology will have probably changed enough to warrant a rebuild.

THE ORIGINS OF THE 9 STEP PROCESS

You will notice that the book's structure is based on the 9 Step Process. This process came about as the result of over a decade of working with agencies from around the U.S. and Canada on marketing sites of all shapes and sizes. Through the three main roles (Attract, Inform, and Engage), we will move horizontally across the process chart pictured on page 14. Following this process allows you to walk through your site planning process in a logical sequence that matches how your prospects will navigate through your website.

Over the years, I have been in contact with thousands of agencies. There was one agency from the Midwest I had been eager to work with for quite a few years. They knew of us, but we had not had any opportunities to work together. One day I received a kind and anonymous tip that this firm was starting to think about rebuilding their own site. I wasted no time in emailing their interactive director, whom I had met a few years prior after my first public speaking opportunity at a small conference in Chicago. As it turned out, not only were they interested in rebuilding their own site, but they were also about to launch a new business for which they needed a site, and they were preparing to pitch a site rebuild to one of their biggest clients.

I found myself sitting in a beautiful historic hotel room in Kansas a few weeks later, excited but fretting about the next day's agenda. The morning would begin with breakfast with two key people from the agency's interactive department, followed by a tour of their office. After that, we would head to the client's office so that I could present to them for an hour and a half, then we'd head back to the agency's office so I could give two presentations, one on marketing firm website best practices and one on planning marketing websites. Looking back, that day still stands out as one of the most intense and enjoyable I've ever had.

The firm's leadership would all be in attendance for the planning presentation, and I only had their attention for thirty minutes. At that point in my career, I had been speaking on web strategy topics for a number of years, but this presentation was going to be a more pointed talk to a more specific group of people in less time than I was used to. I also knew that it was the most important meeting of the day. If that presentation went well, we had a good chance of them choosing to work with us.

So, that night in the hotel room I created the 9 Step Process. It came together quickly, probably due in equal parts to the experiences we have had and the necessity of the situation. The next day, my presentation was successful. The Process was the glue that brought all the otherwise disparate components together. I explained the concepts in much less time than usual, and by the end of the session, it was clear that they had a firm grasp of the material. The fact that we were eventually hired for both jobs was icing on the cake.

Since that day, I have had the opportunity to use this process to explain how marketing websites can work to many dozens of agencies, some who are not sure what a CMS is (CMS stands for Content Management System), and others who regularly do complex web work for huge brands that we all know. In every case, the logic holds and the content is revelatory. I hope the same is true of your experience with this book. < / >

/attract/

IN THIS CHAPTER WE WILL REVIEW:

> How to measure the success of a site
> How SEO really works, and how to optimize a site for search engines
> How to plan for a site that excels at attracting the right prospects

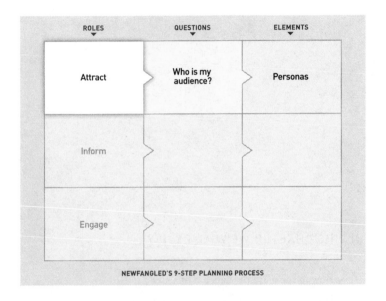

ROLES	QUESTIONS	ELEMENTS
Attract	Who is my audience?	Personas
Inform		
Engage		

NEWFANGLED'S 9-STEP PLANNING PROCESS

Who is my audience?

Traffic is meaningless; action is everything.

Unless you plan to make a lot of money selling ads on your site, traffic is a false measurement of success. The only people you want to spend your resources trying to attract are those who are going to positively impact your business in some way, and there is a tried and true way of doing this.

Only when your site starts generating many high-quality form conversions does it truly begin working for you. At that point, it transforms from a brochure into a real marketing tool.

Attracting the right people to your site is primarily a combined function of your persona development, content strategy, and the way you optimize your site for search engines. If your prospects are not showing up to your site, the quality of the site is irrelevant because no one is listening. Obviously, some prospects, clients, and potential employees who already know about you will find your site one way or another. The main opportunity your site needs to exploit is that of attracting the unaware. Your site needs to be proficient at attracting those who need your expertise but are either unaware you exist or not currently considering you. Preaching to the choir will not hurt, but it also will not affect your business to any measurable degree. That being said, if you create a site that fulfills the goals described in this book, it will surely be a valuable resource for all of your site visitors, regardless of their familiarity with your firm.

This section, which covers SEO (Search Engine Optimization) and persona development, is more technical and implementation oriented than the other sections of the book. Even though these topics are not particularly strategically engaging, it is important to start with them because the first role of the marketing website is to attract the right audience, and that is done specifically through identifying personas and properly optimizing content for those personas and search engines.

Search Engine Optimization

WHAT'S GOOD FOR GOOGLE IS GOOD FOR THE GANDER.
Google has made it simple for us. When talking about SEO, the only SE you really need to consider is Google. They have had over sixty-five percent of the organic search engine market share for the past ten years running (they currently have approximately eighty-four percent). Their sheer popularity is not the main reason that what's good for Google is good for the gander, though. Generally speaking, if you adhere to what Google considers to be SEO best practices, you will be in line with the other major search engines, too.

This is a result of Google's dominance. They set the standards for what a good search engine should be, and most of the others followed suit. Bing is trying to distinctly distance itself from Google by positioning itself as the "answer engine," but the way they index your site is not very different from the way Google does (even though Bing claims to display more accurate results to searchers after gathering larger quantities of information from the web).

So, at the time of this writing, focusing your efforts on attracting Google's interest will result in a well optimized site across all major search engines.

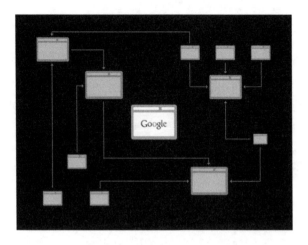

HOW GOOGLE WORKS

Google's mission statement is to "organize all the world's information and make it universally accessible and useful." As a search engine, Google's job is to read the entire web, receive a request from you, and then decide which single page across the pool of the fifteen billion best matches your search. This is a tough job, and Google can only do as good a job as we (those in control of website content) do.

There are two basic parts to the search engine, the bot and the indexer, and they have a bee and hive sort of relationship. The bot is the bee, and it spends all its time reading the internet. It makes no decisions, but simply trolls the internet and collects information. The bot then feeds the indexer (the hive) all the data it has gathered, and the indexer then decides which results should be shown for which searches.

The first step in SEO is ensuring that the bot is interested in reading your site. Since the bot is responsible for reading the internet, it has to make decisions as to where its time is best spent. If you put a new site live today, and the bot indexes it tomorrow, then again in a week, then in three weeks, and then six, and if, each time it visits, it sees that your site has not changed, it will begin to visit your site less frequently.

This principle unfortunately leads people to go into their sites and rearrange the same content in different ways, which brings me to one of the most important points of this chapter.

GOOGLE IS SMARTER THAN YOU ARE.

No matter how intelligent one may be, no one is anywhere close to as smart as Google collectively is—it is not even close. Any "trick" you hear of that entices Google to give your site higher rankings might work well in the short-term, at best. At worst, it will not only never work for you, but it could get your site blacklisted.

So, the next time an SEO expert suggests you put indexable text behind a Flash movie or in a file that loads separately or in the footer of your site with a matching background color or any other equally ridiculous plan, fire them on the spot. They are not smarter than Google.

HOW TO SUCCEED WITH GOOGLE

It always amazes me how many shortcuts people will try in order to do well with Google when Google makes it so easy to succeed if you simply play by the rules. There is one catch, though, and I want to get it out of the way at the outset. *You have to write.* If you regularly add unique, expertise-based content to your site, then SEO will be easy. We will take a close look at how exactly to do this in the content strategy section. If you do not regularly add unique, expertise-based content to your site then doing well with Google is not an option for you and SEO is not worth wasting your time on.

To explain how to properly optimize your site for search engines, it is helpful to outline some of the things not to do. Do not put any content you want Google to read in Flash, documents, or images. Having a PDF download of an article is great, but make sure you also enable people to read that article right there on your site in plain, indexable HTML. When it comes to Flash, be careful, it can do more harm to your site's SEO than anything else. Having a Flash introduction to your site might as well be a "No Trespassing" sign as far as Google is concerned. If your navigation system is in Flash, Google will have a hard time even getting to your site's pages. Flash is also anathema to most mobile devices. If you still consider Flash to be a good idea, I invite you to read my "9 Don'ts of Using Flash" in the Visual Design section.

Assuming your site was built according to coding best practices (a topic that is well understood among most developers and which I will not cover in this book) and that your site is not hiding from Google in any of the ways I just mentioned, SEO is quite easy.

There are three page elements that Google looks at when it examines a single page: the title tag, the URL, and the H1 tag. Let's take a closer look at each:

THE <TITLE> TAG

The title tag is what displays on the very top of the browser bar, above the address bar and everything else. Most people usually waste this space by putting the company name in it or just the title of the page (e.g. "About Us"). This is a waste of this precious space for a few reasons.

Unless your site is a total wreck, people will find you if they enter your company name into Google's search bar. Using this prime real estate to accomplish a goal that you've already met is unnecessary. Using this space to simply mimic the generic title that is already on the page is equally wasteful. You will never have the top search result for the phrase "About Us." Even if you did rank well for such a generic phrase, it is highly unlikely that the searcher was actually looking for a firm like yours, so there is nothing to gain. What, then, should the title tag contain? The answer to this question is one of the most important tactics to use when optimizing for search engines.

THINK LIKE A SEARCHER

How does one think like a searcher? First, read the page you are optimizing, then ask yourself, "What phrase would I use if I were searching for this page on Google?" The resulting phrase is your thesis statement for that page, and it is what you should use as the foundational phrase for these three Google-facing elements.

To further explain this, let's look at a hypothetical firm: one that specializes in packaging design for high-end culinary goods and products. What might the thesis statement be for their "About Us" page? The page's content is about them, and you now know what they do, so an appropriate phrase might be related to their positioning statement. Simply using "packaging design for high-end culinary goods and products" might make sense. It is concise, keyword-rich, expertise-based, and entirely related to the content of that page.

THE URL

The URL, or Uniform Resource Locator, is the page's link, and the URL is one of the opportunities you have (in addition to the <title> and <H1> tags) to let Google know what the page is about.

Too many URLs go wholly unconsidered in terms of their role in the page's SEO. URLs like *http://www.agencysite.com/blog/october/11/showdetails.php?access=1x23f4rIII* are perfectly valid, but perfectly useless for anything but file management. Instead, your URLs should be friendly. A friendly URL looks something like this: *http://www.agencysite.com/packaging-design-for-culinary-products*. Assuming we are talking about the same page as our title tag example, this URL is, once again, concise, keyword-rich, expertise-based, and related to the content of that page. Ask your developer to allow you to have full control over every URL on your site through your CMS and to make sure that the pretty URL is properly paired with its more programmatically useful but less attractive counterpart through 301 redirects.

A 301 redirect is a way for your site to tell search engines that a page at a certain URL has been permanently moved to another URL. For example, when you create a new site, you may switch from an HTML or Flash site to a CMS-based site. This type of switch would most likely mean that all of your pages will have new URLs. *http://www.AgencyWebSite.com/about.htm* might become *http://www.AgencyWebSite.com/about.php*. The difference between those two links may look minimal, but the fact that there is any difference at all means that you need to alert search engines that the content that was on *about.htm* is now on *about.php*, and 301 redirects are the way to do that.

THE <H1> TAG

The H1 tag is one of the first things one comes across when beginning to learn HTML. H1 stands for Heading 1 and is intended to be used to define the topic of the page to the site visitor.

These intentions were created long ago when the web was a very different place, but Google follows these basic rules and looks to the H1 tag in part to initially ascertain what the page is about. The problem is, most developers do not think of the H1 tag in this

way. Instead, they often think of it as a really big headline, and therefore, the H1 tag rarely makes it onto the page; when it does, it is usually misused.

The first thing to do to ensure that you are rolling out the red carpet for Google is to verify that the title on each of your pages that your site visitors read is wrapped in an H1 tag. This title is an important design element since people can look to it to figure out where they are on the site. Designers tend to make this title an image so that they can have unlimited font and styling choices. If the titles of your pages are images, you are missing the boat on a significant SEO opportunity. Font replacement (explained in the Visual Design chapter) makes it easier than ever to use indexable HTML text for your page titles without having to sacrifice font choice.

Of these three Google-facing elements, you may take the most liberties with the H1 tag, as long as you are using the <title> tag and URL effectively. The main reason for this is that the H1 tag is the most conspicuous of the three. People tend to pay less attention to a page's URL and title tag, but everyone sees the title that is on the page. Even though you will use these page elements in part to entice search engines to grant your site preferential rankings, the ultimate point of your site's pages is to serve your visitors well. This distinction is important because it is all too easy to build a site that is so focused on SEO that you lose sight of the fact that the reason you want it to be optimized is to bring the right visitors to your site. If the page in question is about your firm, then "About Us" is a fine H1 tag, even though the title tag is "package design for high-end culinary goods and products" and your URL is */package-design-for-culinary-products*.

The advantage of having three opportunities to describe every page on your site to Google is that you can mix things up. On any given page, you might use the same basic phrase in each of the three elements, you might use a different phrase for each element, or something in between. As long as each phrase is relevant to the content on that page and is considered from the perspectives of both the searcher and the visitor, the page's SEO will be effective.

These tags are your three best opportunities to pique Google's interest in your content. If you craft these elements properly, and the page has at least three hundred to five hundred words of content, chances are good that Google will find the page attractive. If you implement the sort of content strategy I outline later in the book, including adding two thousand words of unique, expert content to your site per month, your site will develop a close and rewarding relationship with Google.

EXPERTISE-BASED SEO

When you combine the approach of "thinking like a searcher" and a content strategy, you take an expertise-based approach to SEO. With the expertise-based approach, you convey to Google who you are in a detailed way on a regular basis. Over time, Google then develops a more accurate idea of whom they should be sending to your site. As you teach Google how to be a better referral agent for your business, Google will respond by bringing the "specific masses" to you. I describe the specific masses as the people from around the world who desire your expertise but either do not yet know you exist or are not currently considering your firm.

An expertise-based approach to SEO, paired with content strategy, makes your site increasingly effective as a marketing tool. The process goes something like this: You add more content to your site that interests your prospects. Google indexes it and brings the right people to your doorstep. Once they arrive, they are convinced of your expertise through the mass of focused educational content that seems to have been written just for them. They identify your site as an educational resource they need, and they act on a call to action form, which is based on your content strategy (e.g. "Sign Up For Our Newsletter").

Furthermore, when your site becomes a plentiful resource, people will start linking to specific pages throughout your site. These links will give Google even more inroads to your content, which will further increase your rankings. Many people make a big deal out of link-building, and some focus more of their attention on figuring out how to have people link to their content than on writing the right content in the first place. While I agree that link-building is an important aspect of SEO, if you focus on writing relevant, expertise-based content, the rest will come.

KEYWORD-BASED SEO

The opposite of expertise-based SEO is keyword-based SEO, and the latter puts your site on a much less advantageous trajectory. Taking a keyword-based approach to SEO looks something like this: You hire an SEO expert. They interview you, ask many useful questions, and then go off and do their research. They come back with a list of the top twenty-five keywords for your firm—the keywords that everyone who wants to hire firms like yours are searching for every day. The idea is that if you could rank well for those keywords, your site would be flooded with hungry prospects. Once you identify these words, the SEO expert then goes about stuffing them into every nook and cranny in your site. They show up in awkward sentences inside of your content; they are in your meta tags (as if they mattered); they are jumbled in a list in your footer; and special secret landing pages are created just to serve as bastions of keyword-rich text that make no sense to anyone. You get the idea.

This approach to SEO is shallow, and it does not work. It may work to get you a decent ranking for those twenty-five phrases in Google, thereby justifying the SEO expert's fees, but once people arrive at your site, you can bet that they will not be persuaded by your keyword-laden marketing speak. The prospects leave, you look shallow, and no one wins. In this scenario, traffic goes up, but the conversion needle doesn't budge.

The truth about SEO is that there is no magic keyword list. Sure, there are important keywords for your firm, but there are thousands of slightly less important keywords that will cumulatively bring in far more people. This fact of SEO is usually referred to as the "long tail" of search.

One example of this "long tail" comes from our own company's website. One of the main pages on our site is the "Planning" page. The title tag is "Web Development Prototyping Process;" the URL is */web_development_prototyping_process*; and the H1 tag is "Planning" (although this is not a perfect SEO keyword, it makes sense from a usability perspective). You might guess that we are interested in ranking well for the phrase "Web Development Prototyping Process," and you would be right. If an SEO expert were going to help us, that phrase would likely be on the list of twenty-five keywords. The facts are surprising, though, and they prove the long tail theory, as do the keyword patterns on all of our pages.

As of this writing, well over two thousand people reached this page on our site through Google alone. What is particularly interesting is that they arrived there through over five hundred different keyword combinations. The partial list you see in the image to the right came directly from our site's statistics, and it shows some of the keywords that have been used to find this page via Google

63	prototyping process website	4
64	web development by prototype	4
65	web development processes	4
66	web page prototype	4
67	website development prototyping	4
68	website prototype process	4
69	website prototyping process	4
70	what is prototyping in web development	4
71	grayscreening	3
72	planning process in prototyping	3
73	process of web prototyping	3
74	prototype development for websites	3
75	prototype for web development	3
76	prototype of a web site	3
77	prototype process development	3
78	prototypes web development	3
79	prototyping for websites	3
80	protyping of the websites	3
81	types of online website prototyping	3
82	web development our process	3
83	web development planning process	3
84	web development prototyping process	3
85	website prototype development tool	3
86	website prototype examples	3
87	website prototyper	3
88	"prototyping process"	2
89	application prototyping process	2
90	web developing prototyping	2
91	basic web development prototyping	2
92	building web prototypes	2
93	built web prototypes	2
94	built website prototype	2
95	develop system using prototyping process	2
96	developing working website prototype	2
97	development of web prototypes	2

(specifically, keywords #63-97 out of 500), and it shows how many times each have been used. This information paints a perfectly clear picture that we will never be able to guess all the ways people will search for our content. The best we can do is tell Google who we are and what we do through our content strategy, frame the pages properly so that it is easy for Google to correctly identify them, and then allow people to find us based on the multiple ways they happen to ask Google questions during their (re)search.

When scanning the list of keyword phrases for our website, you might notice that our highly coveted, silver bullet keyword, "Web Development Prototyping Process," is not the most popular phrase used to access this page. At a lowly ranking of 84th, it is not even close. You will also notice that of the two thousand people who came to this page from Google, only three used this keyword.

THE OPPORTUNITY OF SEO

My favorite thing about SEO is that it is logical. This is not a difficult concept, and anybody with something unique and worthwhile to say can do so and be successful with Google. The fact that the barrier to entry is so low is a great opportunity for you. By implementing these best practices, you can distance yourself from your competitors starting today. Most sites get these basic principles all wrong, so you can have an immediate and significant leg up by going through your site and making sure you are getting them right.

Persona Development

While most of a website's ability to attract attention results from SEO, it is also important to focus on who it is we are trying to attract. Persona development ensures that we focus our SEO, content strategy, and lead generation efforts in the right direction. Even if you know your clients better than you know your family, and even if you have already created client personas, it is still worth taking the small amount of time necessary to create website-specific personas.

Creating personas is one of the most important and overlooked aspects of website planning. Steve Mulder, author of *The User is Always Right*, defines personas as "realistic personality profiles that represent a significant group of your users." It is important to create personas for two basic reasons: one, our sites exist to serve our users, and two, we are, by definition, not our users.

Personas help you to focus on the groups of visitors to your site who matter most; they help you better relate to and understand your visitors; and they help to build consensus among your web planning team. Well-crafted personas serve as a guide for the site development planning stages and are helpful when navigating through the trickier elements of dealing with information design, visual design, call to action creation, and content strategy planning. In the coming pages, I will outline a specific persona development process that is a good mix of what is approachable and useful for marketing websites. For an in-depth guide to persona development for the web, I recommend reading Mulder's book.

When creating personas, a good goal is to come up with about three of them. If you have more than three legitimate and distinct prospect groups, it might be time to reevaluate your firm's market positioning with an eye toward narrowing it. You should allow for roughly two weeks of time for qualitative persona development.

QUALITATIVE PERSONA DEVELOPMENT IN 3 EASY STEPS

Step 1: Research

For qualitative research, you should start by conducting five to ten one-on-one phone interviews. Have a ghost note taker on the line so you can focus on the conversation. Your goal here is to have conversations that eventually touch on a series of points instead of running down a list in a mechanical way. This sort of conversational approach is more likely to encourage the interviewee to open up more freely as you guide the conversation toward your preferred topics. For your candidates, try to choose a wide array of clients and prospects in various buying stages: those who are considering hiring a firm like yours, those who may refer you to others, and those who plan to make a hire in the next year or so. During your conversations, focus on goals, attitudes, and behaviors.

You should have a series of points you try to cover during each conversation so that you have consistent comparison points between conversations and to make sure that you are getting the most out of each call. Mulder has a set list of questions he recommends in his book, but I encourage you to think about creating your own list of questions. What information would help you create a site that attracts, informs, and engages?

This exercise can be an enjoyable and enlightening process. You will be surprised by how much you learn about how your firm is perceived, and the people you speak with will appreciate your considering their opinions. Since you are having meaningful conversations with clients and prospects, the act of doing this research can often be a decent marketing tool in and of itself.

Step 2: Segmentation

Qualitative segmentation is an intuitive and non-scientific process, so go with your gut when creating these segments. The goal is to create three personas, so you should aim for three user segments, and the segments should be based on user goals. Segments might look something like this:

Segment 1: The Skimmer

The Skimmers do not get too deep into details, but they might be interested in looking at the site to make sure the agency does good work and is a legitimate business that deserves attention. They are interested in the portfolio, the principal biographies, and the office locations.

Segment 2: The Researcher

The Researchers do research in order to hire an expert in the industry. They might engage with the site through such calls to action as signing up for newsletters or blogs, registering for webinars or events, or downloading white papers.

Segment 3: The Buyer

The Buyers have done their research, know what they want, and are ready to make a hire. These people would likely either place a call or fill out a project profile.

After you create your segments, test them by asking a specific series of questions. Mulder recommends the following questions:
1. Are the segments unique enough?
2. Do they feel like real people?
3. Can they be easily described?
4. Do they cover all key user types?
5. Is it clear how these segments will affect decision making?

STEP 3: PERSONA CREATION

Once you create your segments, most of the hard work is done. The next step is to create one persona per segment. For each persona,

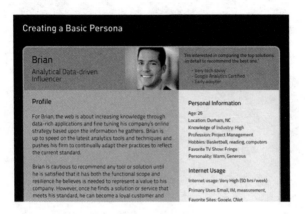

Creating a Basic Persona

Brian
Analytical Data-driven
Influencer

I'm interested in comparing the top solutions in detail to recommend the best one.

- Very tech savvy
- Google Analytics Certified
- Early adopter

Profile

For Brian, the web is about increasing knowledge through data-rich applications and fine tuning his company's online strategy based upon the information he gathers. Brian is up to speed on the latest analytics tools and techniques and pushes his firm to continually adapt their practices to reflect the current standard.

Brian is cautious to recommend any tool or solution until he is satisfied that it has both the functional scope and resilience he believes is needed to represent a value to his company. However, once he finds a solution or service that meets his standard, he can become a loyal customer and

Personal Information

Age: 26
Location: Durham, NC
Knowledge of Industry: High
Profession: Project Management
Hobbies: Basketball, reading, computers
Favorite TV Show: Fringe
Personality: Warm, Generous

Internet Usage

Internet usage: Very High (50 hrs/week)
Primary Uses: Email, IM, measurement,
Favorite Sites: Google, CNet

define specific and realistic attributes, including a fictitious name, title, business, location, age, a believable photo, and a short professional personality description.

As you formulate these attributes, you should also create a cheat sheet for each persona. This should be an actual sheet—something you could print out and share with your web planning team. Precision is more important than accuracy here. Create a sketch of someone who could be a real person. You should also write scenarios for each persona describing who they are, how their problems relate to your services, how they found your site, what calls to action may interest them, and how they would be involved in hiring or referring your firm. </>

/inform/

IN THIS CHAPTER WE WILL REVIEW:

> How to plan an intuitive, highly usable site that hooks
> your prospects
> The balance of power and priority between information
> design and visual design
> How to communicate effectively with your clients throughout
> the web development process
> Print-to-web design tips
> How the modern marketing website works for agencies
> What a content strategy is and how to implement one
> The role of writing in your marketing plan and its benefits

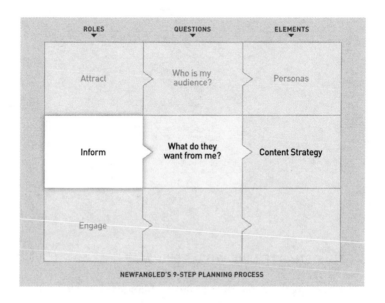

ROLES ▼	QUESTIONS ▼	ELEMENTS ▼
Attract	Who is my audience?	Personas
Inform	What do they want from me?	Content Strategy
Engage		

NEWFANGLED'S 9-STEP PLANNING PROCESS

Now that I have identified exactly what sort of visitor you want to attract and how to lure them to your site through search engines, I will review how to create a site that intuitively leads visitors to the areas most pertinent to them while convincing them of your expertise and creativity along the way.

One of my favorite things about working with agencies is that the events I attend for marketing purposes are also educational events that I would typically want to attend anyway. I always learn a great deal from these events. One such event is the annual New Business Summit, organized by David Baker and Blair Enns, in Nashville. I have taken part in this event five years in a row, the first two as an eager and slightly overwhelmed attendee, and the last three as a just-as-eager speaker. Regardless of how many times I attend the summit, however, I always come away with new and valuable tools.

The first time I attended the New Business Summit in 2005, I heard Blair Enns say that "the purpose of the agency website is to inform and inspire." This resonated with me, and it quickly became a central theme in my perspective on the agency website. Over time, I realized that it is both appropriate and important to bookend "inform and inspire" with "attract" and "engage."

In the 9 Step Process chart, I chose to leave out the inspire part. I did this because I have observed that most agencies already understand that part of the equation quite well. This process is designed to help agencies with the aspects of web development they typically struggle with. While I will present some design ideas and tips in the book, I have neither the need nor the expertise to consult you on how to inspire through your design work.

The elements of your site that are responsible for informing and inspiring are relatively straightforward. The site inspires through its portfolio and informs through its content strategy. The inspiration part comes easily for most agencies since it comes from their creative work. The problem is that many site visitors are unskilled at evaluating design. When comparing two talented agencies, many visitors are unable to readily tell which has the better design. They like both.

The last thing most agencies want is for a contract to be awarded based on the flip of a coin. Fortunately, there is a way to differentiate your site—it isn't easy, but it is necessary. As the inspiration piece comes easily for most firms, the informative piece does not. Informing consists of explaining to your site visitors, by using actual words, why your work is so good. You inform by writing about your expertise. Many people find writing to be quite difficult, but that is why there is such opportunity associated with it; few do it, and even fewer do it well. But I can promise this: the agency that does great work and can explain why it is worthy of a prospect's attention using meaningful, understandable language will consistently beat out the agency that does equally great work but does not take the time to write about the expertise behind the work.

Agencies once had the luxury of being able to explain to a potential prospect what they did and how they did it either in person or over the phone. That first contact was one in which agencies could craft their message specifically for the prospect. Now, however, that level of control is gone. People constantly evaluate your firm based solely on your website.

When presenting these ideas to an agency recently, I displayed an agency site that had been quite successful as a marketing site. The creative director happened to be in the room, and he challenged me on the merits of the site I showed, saying that he thought the particular page I displayed was boring and certainly would not earn the respect of anyone coming to the site and vetting the agency on their creative merits. For me, one of the best parts of giving presentations is the participation from the group to whom I am presenting. The questions, challenges, and affirmations I hear usually end up being the highlights of the talk. In this instance, the creative director's comment offered a great opportunity for me to speak about one of the most subtle, important, and misunderstood details of how the agency website works.

The page I displayed was a blog post, and, as an element of the site's content strategy, its job fell neatly on the "inform" side of things. There will be pages on your site that primarily function to inform, and others to inspire. Agencies frequently believe that every element on every page must exude creativity so that a visitor to the site can admire how much attention they paid to every little detail of their site's design.

The problem with this approach is that all those considered design elements can end up getting in the way of what the visitor is trying to do on your site. I am not saying that the design of your site does not matter. The point is that the site's creativity should not get in the way of the ultimate goal of the site. I recommend viewing your site as a sparse and functional canvas upon which you portray only your best work and most compelling thoughts. Inspire your visitors by the work in your portfolio, but not necessarily by the creativity of the portfolio itself.

Content does not have to be aesthetically boring, does it? Take it as a design challenge to figure out how to make a blog post or a white paper beautiful without distracting from the content. Saying that "we cannot have content pages on our site because they are boring" is not a sustainable excuse.

Beyond the basic point that your site ought to inspire your visitors, it is not my place to tell you how to go about designing your site or its portfolio. The Content Strategy section details exactly how to create a site that excels at informing your site visitors about your firm's expertise.

What does my audience want?

By adding content to your site that describes your expertise in detail, Google can direct the right prospects your way. Those prospects frequently find your site by asking Google many of the marketing questions that confound them. So, what do they want from your site? They want answers. The better a job your site does of answering the questions your prospects have about their marketing problems, the more leads your site will generate. When your site answers their questions, it becomes a valuable educational resource for them. Once they see your site in that light, they are eager to sign up to receive your thought-leadership content on a regular basis through newsletters, blogs, webinars, white papers, e-books, podcasts, and videos.

Your prospects want to be informed and inspired. You inform them through your search engine-friendly content that is based on your expertise and your solutions to your prospects' problems. They are inspired by your work.

In order for your site to succeed in its role of informing, it must be intuitively navigable. When people arrive at your site, regardless of the page on which they initially land, they need to have an intuitive sense of exactly where they are, what the site has to offer, and where they would most like to go.

Information design is the practice through which you ensure that your site operates in this way.

Information Design

When implementing a search engine optimized content strategy on your site, you create a new front door to your site with each article you publish. Because visitors may begin their relationship with you from any page on your site, the site's information design must be flawless. In this section, we will look at how things can frequently go wrong in the design phases of a web project, and we will review a process that allows you to reliably create intuitively navigable sites.

THE MOST IMPORTANT STEP IN THE WEB DEVELOPMENT PROCESS

Information design is the neglected stepchild of web development. This is unfortunate, though, because the truth is that a site's information design is more important than its visual design, content, programming, measurement, calls to action, or anything else. Of course, any good site requires all of those things, but, without the right information design, those elements will not have the structure they need to be effective, and the site will be as weak and precarious as a house of cards.

DON'T LEAD WITH DESIGN

Communicating about the web is hard to do, and many of the agencies I speak with have a hard time figuring out how to build client sites without losing some combination of their reputation, bankroll, and sanity. It does not have to be this way, though. You are capable of putting together a great web project, you just need to have the right process. The main problem we all encounter when approaching a web development project is that a commonsense approach to web development does not work. A good example of this is the way most agencies begin the process of building a website: with design.

Back in Newfangled's early days when I was just learning about sales and how to run client meetings. I noticed that almost every agency I met had the same approach: they wanted to show their clients designs as quickly as possible. Some even wanted to show design before they were hired.

Since we are often involved in the earliest stages of the projects we work on with our agency partners, we used to sit in on a lot of the meetings during which they would "reveal" their initial designs to the client. Before the reveal, both the agency and the client would be excited, but then the agency would show the home page, for example, and the mood in the room would change—usually not for the better.

Prior to that meeting, the client had usually seen very little in the way of information design, maybe a site map, at best. That meant that everything was riding on the homepage that was just revealed. By everything, I mean the client's understanding of the navigation systems, the elements depicted on the homepage, the logo treatment on the web, and even the fonts, colors, imagery, and patterns throughout the site.

The agency had already had the benefit of considering all of these elements one by one and, therefore, had an understanding of how everything related and probably had a vision for how a web user would interact with the designed elements. The poor client, however, saw everything for the first time right then. When the client saw the homepage, they worried about how much of the design budget this represented, what their boss would think of it, and how their response would affect the agency (who was clearly looking for some immediate input), all while trying to process the hundreds of big and small decisions the agency made during the design creation process. The cumulative weight of all of these questions is enough to make anyone short-circuit from information overload. In those sessions, we knew the client's mind went AWOL when they said something like, "The CEO doesn't like blue."

I have heard many agencies complain that their web projects fail because their clients cannot make up their minds about anything and are continually contradicting themselves. These agencies are not delusional; their clients really are giving them lousy feedback. But it is not the client's fault, it's the agency's.

Clients hire you because they cannot build their website themselves. They need you to expertly guide them through the difficult and unintuitive web development process. As a guide, it is one of your responsibilities to never give your clients more information than they can process. You should always put them in situations in which they can succeed. They will only be successful if you can give accurate and timely feedback, so the onus is on you to show them only as much as they can comprehend and respond to promptly.

The client in the above scenario would not be able to ignore the currently "unimportant" elements of the page and just give feedback on the design. It does not matter how often or emphatically you tell them to look here and not there. They are going to look everywhere. When you lead with design, clients will instinctively look at everything but the design elements. "Is that what our main navigation should be?", "Do we really want a picture of Herb on the homepage?", and "Where's the mission statement we just spent the past ten months writing?" are examples of things that race through your client's head when you overwhelm them with a design-first approach to web development.

You should lead clients in a logical and consistent way through the web development process, and there is only one place to start: information design. Information design comes first, and visual design comes second.

A WALK IN THE WOODS

To take a look at why a site's information design is so important, let's step away from the web for a moment. Say it is a beautiful Sunday afternoon in the fall, and you decide to go for a walk in the woods. Now consider two basic types of walks, one successful and one not. On the successful walk, you start at the trailhead, make your way onto the trail, and meander along, stopping here and there to enjoy the foliage. Eventually, you follow the trail markers back to the trailhead. The walk concludes, and your body and mind are all the better for it.

Conversely, what if, halfway through the walk, you realize you have not seen a trail marker in a little too long? Within moments, your heart and mind switch into survival mode, and before you know it, your pleasant walk is over. Your only care is to get out of these weird, spooky woods and back to your car right away.

The Website Development Process

The image above describes the way I would suggest you stage your web development process.

YOUR HOME PAGE IS NOT YOUR HOME PAGE

The same type of thing is true when we navigate websites. Because many of us arrive on sites after being referred to a specific page through a search engine, we often find ourselves on some low-level page far, far away from that home page everyone so carefully considered when the site was being built.

Because of our search-based leanings, you must consider every page of your site to be its home page. Ask yourself, "What would I think of this site if I landed, sight unseen, on the third page of that archived newsletter from February 2005, or the fifth brochure page of the oldest case study in the portfolio? Would I have an intuitive sense of where I am in the greater context of the site? Would I know who my company is, what we do, and what other areas of the site I should visit, all without leaving the current page?"

If the site you currently have or are building passes this test, then its information design is functioning well. Most sites, however, do not pass this test. They fail because agencies and web developers do curious things like rush through the information design stage to get started on the visual design. Discovering a site's perfect information design is essential and not difficult to do if you create the right conditions for it.

WHAT IS INFORMATION DESIGN?

A site's information design consists of three elements:

1. The pages on the site
2. The navigation systems that connect all of the pages
3. The elements that are on each page

What is not part of the information design is approved content and visual design. When planning your site's information design, it is important to exclude any visual design elements. Your information design document should be as visually bland as possible, so as to neither limit the freedom of the designer once the project moves on to the design stage nor confuse the client (even if that client is you). At this stage, we are not talking about images, fonts, colors, relative proportions, or anything of the sort. In terms of copy, good old fashioned greeking is just fine in most cases. When discovering a page's information design, it is not important whether or not the copy on the page is approved; all we care about is whether there will be copy and roughly how many paragraphs of it there will be.

AVOIDING MEDIA MISCOMMUNICATION

Many agencies try to communicate with their clients about what kind of website they plan to build using absolutely any means possible other than the web. They make site maps and wireframes using sticky notes, PDFs, spreadsheets, power point presentations, binders full of paper—you name it. The flaw in this approach is that it tries to describe a product that will eventually exist in the nonlinear web medium with an inherently linear paper medium. When the media are at odds, miscommunication is guaranteed. What can be so frustrating about this process is that, despite trying their best to communicate with their clients, agencies frequently recognize that miscommunication is taking place, but they are just not sure where. These types of projects are marked by a tense buildup to the time the site is almost complete, at which point the client can finally interact with the site using a mouse, screen, and keyboard for the first time. It is only at that moment when the agency knows for sure if they were successful or not. This is a scary and precarious way to run a web project. Websites often take around three to five months to complete, which is a long time to live in this kind of fear. In this scenario, though, the agency is not the only one who has been afraid for the past five months.

Almost all of your prospective clients have been through at least one or two web development projects, and chances are good that those projects did not go well. Why should they believe their experience with you will be any different? You said the right things in the sales meetings, but so did the last agency. Your client can sense if you are not genuinely confident about what you are doing, and if you do not have faith in your process, neither will they. From the moment they sense your fear, every conversation you have with them will be increasingly unproductive and contentious.

This dynamic plagues the majority of web projects and is the number one reason they fail. In web projects, you can only lead effectively if you are confident that you will get the job done right the first time. You cannot have that confidence unless you know you are effectively communicating with your client. If your communication is not perfect—especially at this crucial information design planning stage—the web project may be in jeopardy.

GRAYSCREEN PROTOTYPING

At Newfangled, we had to learn this lesson and discover this process the hard way. After building a site that did not meet client expectations one too many times from 1995-2000, we had an important but seemingly futile epiphany. We realized that we could solve most of our communication problems if only we could build the site twice. We could build the site the first time, let the client interact with it, gather all their feedback, and then build it a second

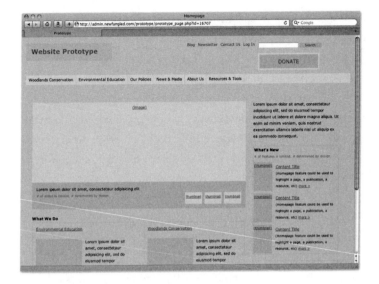

time to their exact specifications. Surely that would be a foolproof process! The only hangup was that no client would be willing to pay twice as much and wait twice as long for their site.

The solution to this problem is grayscreen prototyping. Grayscreen prototyping allows you to create grayscale web pages that mimic the pages of the site you are planning without doubling the budget or timeline. These pages are interactive wireframes, free of any real imagery, design, or content. They exist solely for your clients to interact with their information design document via the web medium. Using one of the many inexpensive grayscreen prototyping tools available (such as Protoshare), you can create an initial grayscale version of a site in a few hours, and it is easy to add, edit, and delete pages at will throughout the information design process.

A SUGGESTED PROTOTYPING PROCESS

The length of the prototyping stage of the web development process is usually about one-third of the entire project. If the project is in the typical three to five month range, prototyping will probably take four to six weeks.

You can start a prototype with a basic sitemap, either one you create after going through the 9 Step Process or one that the client supplies. Either way, the sitemap should just be a rough sketch of the site's navigation. No one should spend much time on it, and it certainly should not go through any rounds of approval. This is because all you really want from the sitemap is a starting point, and given the effect prototyping usually has on site maps, it will be a starting point that you quickly leave behind.

Once the basic prototype is built from the sitemap, it is time to start the revision process, which will take you through to the end of the prototyping stage. You can, of course, approach this however you like, but we find it to be useful to have two prototyping meetings per week (per site). A session usually lasts an hour and includes the project teams from both the agency and the client. The agency leads the meetings and makes the updates to the prototype.

In terms of the order, I suggest working on the navigation systems first [main, secondary, tertiary, and then auxiliary (breadcrumb, global, footer, etc)]. Once all the site's pages have been defined, you can then move on to prototyping out the elements on each page. This requires a discussion about each page, or at least each type of page, on the website. You can deal with some pages, like "Privacy Policy," quickly, but other page types, such as complex product detail pages, may individually require a few hour-long sessions to work through.

If the idea of taking a few hours to talk through the logic of a particular page sounds intimidating, think of how many ways you could get that page wrong if you do not spend the time to talk through its workings with the client. It is worth noting that working through difficult information design problems at this stage is far easier than trying to work with a client to re-architect a page that has been failing them on a live site. Prototyping does not eliminate these sorts of failures, but it greatly reduces them. This is work that has to be done sooner or later, and the earlier in the process you and the client discover and deal with these issues, the easier it will be to work through them.

The prototype is complete once you and the client document every type of page a site visitor might see. I recommend working through all the navigation first, and then working through the page details section by section, starting with the most complicated sections, and then asking the client for final and formal approval on the entire prototype once it is finished. Let them know that this approval is meaningful. After the prototype is approved, any changes to structure or functionality defined in the prototype would constitute a billable change of scope.

This is an important line to draw. The information design process precedes visual design, content creation, and programming because it provides the rule book for the people doing all three of those things. If the rule book changes after the prototype has been approved, there is a lot of work to redo, most likely by all three roles. When you stop trying to explain the web with print and drop traditional wireframes and site maps in favor of grayscreen prototypes, virtually all of your client communication issues about the web project disappear, and you can begin to have focused and effective conversations with your clients about information design.

Instead of badgering them to approve version 2C, rev. 4 of a site map, you can have interesting debates about which solution to a specific information design problem is best. The conversation changes from "approve this" to "let's prototype a few possible solutions so that we can find the best one together." Where the old "approve this" approach built anxiety and mistrust in your clients, the new conversations will build trust, understanding, and excitement.

Furthermore, since your clients can interact with the prototype, they can observe and enjoy the tangible work you do for them at the earliest stage of the project. Between having the sense that you communicate about their needs in an effective and self-documenting way, and seeing such clear proof that you get a lot of work done quickly, your clients can relax early on in the development process.

What happens when they relax? They start thinking more clearly, having better ideas, and being more valuable brainstorming partners. In short, they become good clients.

There are many great books written solely about web site planning, and often the web developer with whom you work helps to guide this stage of the process. It is your job as the agency to give the information design discovery and planning stage of your web development project the time and attention it requires. If you get the right information design in place, you will have a stable foundation upon which to design a first-rate, effective website.

Visual Design

THE BASIC PRINCIPLES OF EFFECTIVE WEB DESIGN

Because Newfangled has done so much work with agencies over the past fifteen years, I have learned a lot about the print to web transition. While I have written about this topic and given many lectures on it around the country, I do not intend to rehash all of the print to web design rules here. There are a few basic points I will cover in the context of this book, however.

IT'S A WEBSITE, NOT A MAGAZINE AD.

The most common mistake agencies make when approaching web design is that they cannot seem to help but treat it like a print design piece. I believe that good agencies and good designers have all the skills they need to be good web designers, but they need to have a different approach.

As Chris Butler wrote in one of our newsletters on design, "Print design is like classical composition, and web design is like jazz." Classical composers meticulously place every note for every instrument in an intentional spot. The pieces are faithfully reproduced by well-trained musicians (think: printers) time and time again. Compositions created hundreds of years ago are still performed with little variance today. Print also works this way. You design the perfect ad, send it over to the printer, review the details, get a spec version, approve it, and then ten thousand copies appear on your doorstep a few weeks later, never to be changed.

In terms of process and expectations, web design could not be more different from print. The web, after all, is like jazz. Even the most brilliant jazz composers almost never set out to craft every note every musician would play. In fact, most jazz songs are never played the same way twice. The band leader sets a musical melody or motif, and then the band gathers around that motif for a few measures. From there, each musician gets a solo section during which they impart their own character, the band comes back together at the end to voice the motif again, and the song is done. This is a bit of a simplification, but, essentially, that is how it goes.

Much like a jazz song, the web is never the same way twice, and this is a fact you must be cognizant of, play to, and design in harmony with. The main thing to focus on is relinquishing control. A web page's design cannot be successfully micromanaged. Even if you do create the perfect design where every element is in perfect harmony, what happens when the client logs in to the CMS to add two more paragraphs and three new images to the page? What happens when fourteen people add blog comments to the bottom of the page? What happens when a visually impaired person ratchets up the font size of the browser to read the page?

These are questions better answered pre-design than post-design. Consider the user. Consider the medium. Be confident in your design skill, and leave your need for complete control at the door.

Whenever you try to impose your print designer's will on a web page, you undoubtedly create a page that is not as user-friendly or successful as it ought to be. Sorry for the tough love here, but you will not create a design that is so amazing that it will change the way everyone uses the web. The best thing you can do to create noteworthy web designs and to be an expert web designer is to play to the well-established truths of web design. Discovering and designing to the limitations of any medium is the hallmark of a great artist. In most cases, even those artists who do break the rules do so only after developing a masterful understanding of what the rules were in the first place. Web design is evolving, for sure, but the people who push the boundaries are those who understand the medium well, not print designers who try to apply their knowledge of one medium to another. Experienced users can spot those people from a mile away, and you do not want to be put in that category. Here are a few common pitfalls to avoid.

DESIGNING IN A BOX

One common example of not playing to the truths of web design is designing a site that is stuck within a fixed-sized box. There are scroll bars here, there, and everywhere which allow content and site features to be scrolled through inside of the box, but the site is locked in to a set size on every page. Whenever I see that, I have no doubt that a print designer was at work.

One reason designers do this is to ensure that everything will be above the fold. Here is a tip: forget about the fold. Web users scroll. Before the invention of the scroll wheel on the mouse, there was an argument to be made against this, but those days ended long ago. Mobile devices have solidified the issue by making things even more intuitive by finger scrolling and swiping directly on the screen.

You are designing a website, not a newspaper, and while it is important to keep certain site utilities, such as the main navigational elements, the search interface, and the calls to action, within the top eight hundred pixels or so, it is no problem to let the content of the page flow on down. The modern web user does not mind this, and you will probably grow to like it, too, if you haven't already.

WHAT ABOUT FONTS?

Unfortunately, there are still only a small number of web-safe fonts, and this is certainly a design limitation we could live without. Fortunately, there are now alternatives. Throughout this book, I do a good deal of Flash-bashing, but here finally is an example of when Flash is useful: font replacement.

sIFR and cufon are two tools that use the Flash font library to swap out boring old Helvetica for something far more interesting and appropriate. Now, before you go thinking that all is well in the world, I need to point out that you should not do this type of font replacement for all of the text on your site.

The way Flash-based font replacement works is that when a web page is loading and the browser gets to the portion of the page that declares the font replacement, Flash's font engine loads, it identifies the correct font, and that text is displayed in that font via the browser. This sounds more complicated than it is, but all of those steps—particularly the Flash font library loading part—take time. If you did this for all the text on a page, it would create a very slow page load time, and this of course is not advisable.

Font replacement is a great technique to use sparingly for key page elements, such as titles, subtitles, and captions.

sIFR and cufon work well, but @font-face is probably the best way of displaying fonts, since it does not rely on either Flash or javascript. Because of this, you can use it more liberally throughout the site. @font-face works with CSS, and you can either purchase it or find it in free font libraries. You define the location of the font library through the @font-face style, and you can then call that named library through any of your other CSS styles.

This font issue is a great example of the continually evolving web landscape. When I started writing this book a year ago, @font-face, CSS3, and HTML 5 were not quite ready for prime time due to a lack of browser support. Today, though, it looks like @font-face will, or at least should, replace the use of sIFR and cufon.

USING FLASH

Based on the list to the right, it probably looks like I do not believe you should use Flash at all on your site, but that is not my intent. Using Flash elements on certain pages can be a powerful addition as long as you are mindful of exactly who might not be able to see or find that content.

FUN WITH NAVIGATION

After "Designing in a Box," getting creative with navigation is the next most common print to web misstep I see agencies make. Designers often want their site to make a splash, so to speak, and a great number of print-turned-web designers use their site's navigation to make their creative mark.

The 9 Don'ts of Using Flash
In describing how to use Flash appropriately, it makes more sense to first describe what not to do.

- Don't have a Flash intro to your site.
- Don't have a Flash-based navigation system.
- Don't build your entire site in Flash.
- Don't put any content you'd like people to find through search engines in Flash.
- Don't put any important site utilities in Flash.
- Don't put anything you'd like a visitor on a mobile device to see in Flash.
- Don't put any site elements that need to meet basic accessibility or usability standards in Flash.
- Don't put anything that you'd like to be able to easily update through a CMS in Flash.
- Don't use Flash when JQuery will do.

This is a problem because the users of your site are seldom concerned with how creative your site is (although they most certainly are interested in the work displayed on the site), and a site's navigation system is its roads and streets. How much did you enjoy the "creativity" of the city planner the last time you were lost in a busy downtown that had an illogical street grid? Not so much, I imagine.

If demonstrating creativity is one of the primary jobs of the site on which you are working, then it is advisable to do so only in certain areas (such as the portfolio or marquees on key pages) and not make the site a guessing game for your users.

MOOD BOARDS

A useful strategy for communicating website plans with your in-house team or client is to separate the discussions about information design from those about visual design. This is helpful for both seasoned professionals and web neophytes.

In the previous section, we looked at information design, commonly referred to as a site's information architecture. A site's information design is composed of the pages on the site, the navigation systems that connect all the pages, and the elements that are on each page.

Using mood boards is a pre-design planning phase for a site's visual design, much like grayscreen prototyping is a pre-programming planning phase for a site's information design.

Communicating with your clients about their website's design can be difficult because they rarely understand design for the web and, therefore, do not know how to talk about it. It is easy for a client to take a position on which pages the site needs to have, what the form fields on the contact page are, and what calls to action should be on the product pages. However, when you start asking them about fonts, patterns, and imagery, things can get a little dangerous. At best, they clam up and offer you very little. At worst, they tell you that the boss loves comic sans and bright orange.

Your clients hire you because they know they cannot and should not design the website themselves. They need you to guide them through the design process. What they need, more than anything, is for you to clearly communicate with them about their site's design so that they can understand what you are doing, why you are doing it, and provide you with useful feedback along the way.

Jumping right into home and sub page designs is too much of a leap for most clients, even though it seems like the obvious thing to do. When you jump right into page design decisions, the client often wants to talk about the things with which they are familiar, and they go back to talking about non-visual elements, such as page names, navigation, and the like. Ideally, you will have already gone through a thorough information design planning stage with the grayscreen prototype. Now, you need to focus the conversation on the visual design, and mood boards are just the thing.

Mood boards deal only with the visual design elements. In the mood board example above, you can see that mood boards look sort of like a web page in their basic dimensions and proportions, but beyond the logo, there are no typical web page features—no navigation, no links, and not even set text. Instead, mood boards focus on the fonts, imagery, color palettes, and textures for the website. Each of these elements are defined by name on the mood board itself. By doing this, you force the conversation to focus on these elements alone, and you give the client the terms to use to discuss them with you.

In terms of process, I recommend posting two to three distinct mood boards, working with the client to choose one direction, and then going through another round or two of revisions against the chosen direction.

If the design directive provided by the client is distinct and there is little room for creativity or inspiration, this pre-design planning stage might be overkill. Otherwise, I would not give up mood boards for anything.

A NOTE ON THE WEB DESIGN PROCESS

The project should have momentum by the time you get to the point of creating home and sub page design comps. If you follow the process described in the past two sections, you will have a detailed, clickable, and approved prototype that clearly defines the site's information design, and you will have approved mood boards that define the basic components of the site's visual design.

By following these two steps, you create little chance for miscommunication or surprise in your discussions with your client about the design and functionality of the site. The client should not be blown away by your home page and sub page comps. They are simply the next logical step in an iterative and calculated progression of communication about the website you are creating. This does not mean that your designs will not be impressive, it simply means that it is unlikely that the client will be shocked at any point in the process.

I know that this is going to be a downer for quite a few designers. The moment when they reveal their design can be a thrilling one. That is, as long as the client responds favorably. However, the truth is, clients generally do not like surprises, and they are ill-equipped to deal with them. As a result, these types of "reveals" can often end with both the designer and client leaving the meeting with more questions (and frustration) than they had when they arrived.

I offer a different reveal as an alternative, and we have seen time and again through our experience in working with agencies that this one is a lot more gratifying. As opposed to having the climax of the project occur when the designs are revealed (usually in an early stage of the project), what if it happens when a site goes live and is a profitable piece of work that the client loves, the agency loves, and prospects flock to? That sort of reveal is much more appropriate and gratifying. If you follow this process, it is also something that can be achieved with predictable and repeatable success, unlike the way a design reveal may be received.

Content Strategy

A content strategy is a plan for regularly adding unique, expert, and indexable content to your site.

After you complete the "Attract" exercise of planning your personas, you have a good idea of what kind of resource your site should be, and this is one of the two things you need to know to plan your content strategy. The second thing you need is a sober and realistic understanding of what sort of content strategy you can commit to, long-term.

When planning their sites, many businesses invent time in their future schedules. They believe that they will suddenly have time, as a firm, to create monthly newsletters, weekly blog posts, quarterly webinars, occasional white papers, and take part in speaking engagements, too. Going from zero to sixty in a few short months is unadvisable, if not impossible.

Many agency sites do not yet implement a content strategy. If you are just getting started on yours, I highly recommend picking one content strategy platform and doing it well. Once you are comfortable with that first platform and can prove a commitment to the writing schedule it requires, you might consider expanding your content strategy.

As long as you add roughly two thousand words of unique, search engine-indexable content that is based on your expertise to your site each month, you should start to see a positive improvement in your site's ability to generate leads.

THE MODERN MARKETING WEBSITE

What if you could speak with every prospect who was considering hiring your firm? And what if they did not just have thirty minutes or so to speak with you, but instead they had all the time in the world—however long it took you to show them how great your agency is? What would you want to do with that time?

You would want them to get to know you, so that they have a sense of the firm's vision and the pace being set by the leadership. You would show them your work, taking them through specific examples, explaining to them what the unique challenges were for certain projects and how you solved them. You would probably want to introduce them to your key employees, let them sit with each one and get to know who they are, what they think about, and see ways in which they have helped similar clients. At the end of their visit, you would want to establish ways in which the two of you could keep in touch on a regular basis. You might make promises to let them know when your next project launches or when you publish your next white paper.

Agencies do not tend to think this way because they logically think that no legitimate early stage prospects could give each agency they review that sort of time. Before the web, this was mostly true, but now this is exactly what happens—or, rather, what could happen if your website were up to the job. Think about it. Would someone visiting your site today be able to do everything I just mentioned above? If so, you have a healthy modern marketing website. If not, it is time to get to work.

There are two absolutely necessary ingredients for creating a modern marketing website for your firm: a commitment to specialization and a commitment to writing.

If you are not specialized, you are not saying anything different from any other agency out there, so your writing efforts will not get you far. If you are specialized, but you do not write, no one will be able to discover you. Even if they do happen to stumble upon your site, there will not be enough there to back up your claims of specialization, and your visitors may not trust you.

Although I do not detail the importance of specialization in this book, I should explain what I mean by it. Your specialization is defined by your focused expertise, which is defined by your positioning statement, which should be prominently placed on your home page. If your positioning statement says that your agency is "a full-service agency that is passionate about creating breakthrough brands that last," then you might want to cut to the chase and be more direct with your site visitors by simply saying that you are "a typical agency that does the same thing everyone else does."

A truly specialized firm would be one like the one I used in the example in the SEO section that strictly focuses on "packaging design for high-end culinary products." That firm knows what size containers of sea salt sell best at which online and offline stores and which weight paper stock gives the customer the feeling that this one pound bag of organic artisinal pasta really is worth eight dollars. That agency knows these details, and every job they work on makes them smarter about a very specific industry segment. They have a lot to write about, and when the right prospect gets caught in the expertise-based content web of their site, that prospect's business becomes theirs to lose. Specialization is not easy, and it requires taking risks and making sacrifices, but the fact is that creating a truly differentiated product or service is the first step in marketing anything. But, hey, you have an advertising agency, you already know that. You would not want to take on a client who does the same thing as all of their competitors, would you?

Content strategy fuels the modern marketing website. While having a deep well of industry-specific knowledge to pull from is essential, that is only half the battle. If you want your knowledge to be a marketing asset that works for you every hour of every day, your site needs to be a robust, relevant, and accurate reflection of your firm's expertise.

In order for a prospect to find you, your site needs to have a wealth of unique and search engine-indexable content. Once a prospect arrives, the job of the site is to take them on a tour that showcases who you are, what you do, what you think about, why you are or are not the right fit for them, and what steps they can take to get to know you better. That is a lot of work for your site to do, and accomplishing this is no small

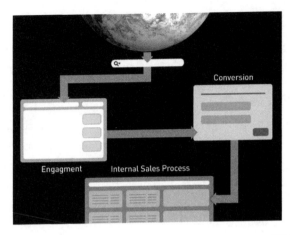

The Website Lead Cycle: From the Outside World to Your CRM

feat. The only way your site can do an accurate and consistent job of this is if you are constantly feeding it with your firm's best and most current thought. Your content strategy is the vehicle for that thought.

WHAT IS A CONTENT STRATEGY?

Once again, the definition of a content strategy is "a plan for regularly adding unique, expert, and indexable content to your site." There are many types of content strategies, but in this book I outline a website-based marketing content strategy. This sort of content usually takes the form of blogs, newsletters, white papers, webinars, videos, and podcasts. This is a detailed and intentional definition, so I will break it down part by part.

A PLAN FOR *REGULARLY* ADDING...

Whenever I discuss content strategy with agencies, one of the first questions that comes up is, "What does adding content to my site on a regular basis really mean?" The answer to this depends on which content strategy platform(s) you choose because different platforms come with different standard expectations for frequency of publication. Later in this section, I review the most popular content strategy platforms (newsletters, blogs, and webinars) and the frequency of publishing associated with each. In general, though, it is a good rule of thumb to plan to add at least two thousand words of content to your site each month (firm-wide), possibly broken up over the span of two to four articles. As long as the quality remains high, more is better, but a two thousand word per month benchmark is a sufficient starting point.

Depending on your experience, this may or may not sound like much writing to you. If you already have the knowledge that comes with specialization, it should not take any more than ten to fifteen hours each month to write, publish, and distribute two thousand words of copy. This time will obviously increase in proportion to the amount of research you need to do for each article. It is not a bad idea to mix things up, writing some articles based on your core knowledge and others that require more outside observation and research. Different people inside your firm may be drawn to different styles of writing in this way, which brings us to an important point.

Since one of the main goals of your content strategy is to reflect the expertise of the firm, it makes sense that multiple people inside of the firm contribute to it on a regular basis. This gives your prospects a more well-rounded understanding of the firm and offers a greater level of transparency and insight into your culture and what it might be like to work with you.

A PLAN FOR REGULARLY ADDING *UNIQUE, EXPERT...*

The content you add should be written by your firm, based on your detailed expertise, as an educational resource for your prospects. Your site ought to be a wealth of information for the audience you serve. Do you know that feeling you get when you search on Google for something, and you finally find that site that not only answers the immediate question you asked, but so many other questions you had over the years as well? That is how you want your prospects to feel when they find your site.

Through your content strategy you should describe your firm's expertise as clearly and openly as possible. You want to be generous with the knowledge you share through your site's content strategy. This idea makes many agencies feel uncomfortable in two ways.

First, they worry that if they give away too much on their site, their clients will no longer need to hire them. We have found this to be absolutely untrue. One reason for this is that although you share your knowledge in your content strategy, you are not applying that knowledge to specific client problems. This allows you to demonstrate your intelligence without obviating the need for your clients to hire you. The other thing that happens when you describe your expertise in detail is that your prospects realize just how complicated the situation really is; they realize that there is a lot more to a perfect marketing solution than just a new coat of paint.

Second, agencies worry that if they put too much of their knowledge on their site, their competitors will steal their ideas. This one is partially true. The term "thought leader" implies that there are followers. Who would you rather be, the leader or the follower? When you are a leader, the followers are usually your competition. While it is possible that your competitors may borrow a few ideas from your site now and then, the value of the impression your site makes on your prospects far outweighs the danger of someone stealing a particular nugget of thought. Mimicry, to a certain extent, is the price a thought leader pays for being at the forefront of their industry. Most well-educated prospects can tell the original from the fake, especially once they speak to both firms. If the prospect is aware enough to realize that Agency B is borrowing your content, your position gets elevated even higher. That being said, I have not seen this scenario happen very often. The agency world is a small one, even more so for specialized agencies, and few agencies are shameless enough to steal content and publish it in a format as public as a website.

A PLAN FOR REGULARLY ADDING UNIQUE, EXPERT, AND *INDEXABLE* CONTENT...

Indexable means that search engines can easily discover and read the content. In order to do so, the content cannot be hidden inside an image, a Flash movie, a PDF file, or behind a login. The content, in full, needs to be right there on the page for the world to see. Not putting your content in Flash or images is easy enough for most agencies these days, but the other two obstructions usually raise a few questions.

Having your content in a PDF file is great, as long as the entirety of the content is also on the web page. Some of your visitors may be more likely to download a PDF, possibly print it, and read it on their own time rather than reading the content through a browser on your site. I am all for allowing people to consume your content on their terms. You just want to make sure that any content that is in a PDF is also presented on your site to visitors and search engines alike in an indexable format. A quick trick you can use to tell if your content is indexable is to start at the top of a paragraph, click, and then drag your mouse to the end of that paragraph. If the text highlights, it is indexable.

The more common objection I hear has to do with putting content behind a login. If your site visitors cannot read your content without logging in or submitting some sort of form, that means Google cannot see it either. Many agencies (and businesses in general) want their visitors to log in to access content so that they can see who is reading what and to gather lead information. If your site already receives all the traffic you could ever want, this might be a good way to go (maybe). Most small agency sites, however, average well below one hundred unique visitors per day and, therefore, are not receiving enough traffic to afford the freedom to take this approach. There is a truth of people's online user behavior that makes this point moot, anyway.

If your visitors find your content engaging enough that they are willing to take the time to fill out a form, they are more likely to do so for the convenience of automatically receiving your content (e.g. Subscribe to Our Newsletter) than they would be to have the privilege of reading your content in the first place (e.g. Log In to Read the Article). A site that publishes all of its content for the world to read and for search engines to index, unencumbered, will bring in far more traffic and capture far more total leads than a site that hides everything behind a login. The golden rule here is to be generous with your content strategy.

A PLAN FOR REGULARLY ADDING UNIQUE, EXPERT, AND INDEXABLE CONTENT TO *YOUR SITE*.

This point mostly pertains to blogs. Many agency blogs exist outside of their site. This usually happens because the agency did not consider including a blog on their site during their last redesign, and it is so darn easy and cheap to install a blog, set it up under *blog.agencywebsite.com*, and make it look sort of like the main site. The blog is literally tacked on to the site. Since many people do it, it may seem that this practice is just fine. It's not.

So many agencies' blogging strategies go awry when they put the blog—and all that great blog content—on a separate site. This is a problem for two distinct and important reasons. The first is that you want your prospects on your site, period. You want them to be able to land on a blog post via a Google search, discover that you are smart and worth examining, and then jump easily right into your portfolio, sign up for your newsletter, contact one of the principals, or forward the post to a friend—all within one click from the page on which they initially landed. If the blog is on one site, and all or some of those things are on another site, you miss the main benefit of any work you do on the blog.

Agencies sometimes think they solve this problem by putting prominent links back and forth from their main site to their blog site. A quick look at your analytics account will show you that most people do not go from your blog back to your main site.

The second reason that separating the two sites is a problem has to do with search engine optimization. While Google is smart enough to understand that *blog.agency.com* is related to *agency.*

com, nothing beats having all of your content under one single domain. This argument, coupled with the first argument, leaves us with few reasons to keep the sites separate. In fact, when it comes to content strategy for marketing firms, I cannot think of a single one.

WHY WRITE?

The act of writing on a regular basis is the only thing standing between your site being what it is today and being the sole source of twenty percent of your closed new business. At Newfangled, we keep close track of how much time we spend on our content strategy and where our business comes from. We did not pull this twenty percent number out of thin air. It is a real number based on our experience. This is not due to our locations, the sort of work we do, or the types of clients we have. Instead, it has to do with the fact that we are sharply positioned and disciplined with our content strategy.

Because writing is so hard for almost every agency, those who do commit to a long-term content strategy separate themselves from the pack. Sure, writing is difficult, but no one said marketing was easy. You understand that you have to market your firm, you understand that your website is your best opportunity to do that and the best way to make your site the strongest marketing resource possible is through its content strategy. Here are four reasons to start writing for your content strategy today.

1. WITHOUT A CONTENT STRATEGY, YOUR SITE IS A BROCHURE.

This one is clear. You can have a brochure, or you can have a modern marketing website that is a lead-generation machine. The difference between the two is a well-executed content strategy.

2. WHEN IT COMES TO SEO, AGE MATTERS.

Say you start your content strategy today, and say that in maybe six months your competitor realizes that you trounce him on all the search phrases for which the two of you have always competed. Maybe, at that point, he is smart enough to realize that you are winning because of your content strategy, so he starts one, too. Google knows that you have been adding two thousand words per month to your site for six months longer than he has. You literally have a six month, twelve thousand word advantage on this competitor. All other things being equal, you will still beat him for like phrases.

Granted, there are other factors at play in a search engine's algorithm, but Google is kind of like Santa in that it knows what you have been doing. If you embark on your firm's content strategy today, you could very well dominate the search engine rankings for your space before your competition knows what hit them. This assumes that your firm is well-positioned. The more similar your expertise is to other agencies, the more difficult your competition will be across the board, and this applies to SEO as well.

3. YOUR CONTENT STRATEGY MAKES YOU SMARTER.

The objective of your content strategy is to make your site into an educational resource for your prospects, but you are the person who stands to learn the most from it.

Humans learn by communicating. You may know everything there is to know about a particular topic, but you cannot fully master it until you learn how to teach that knowledge to somebody else. The act of figuring out how to effectively explain your expertise to someone else increases your mastery of the material significantly. The blog post you write in the morning will enable you to present that topic more eloquently during your new business conversation that afternoon. Teaching others helps us recognize patterns in our own knowledge and connect ideas that bring the big picture into greater focus for ourselves and our readers. Being intelligent is one thing, but being able to communicate your intelligence is altogether different. It may surprise you to see how your involvement in your firm's content strategy sharpens your communication and sales skills.

4. THE CONTENT YOU CREATE IS REPURPOSEABLE AND LEADS TO OPPORTUNITY.

Different prospects will want to consume your content in different ways. Some people would rather watch a thirty minute webinar over lunch than spend ten minutes reading a newsletter over coffee in the morning. Others would rather spend three minutes a day over the course of five days reading the same material in a series of blog posts through their RSS reader. The point is, just because you wrote a newsletter on a certain topic should not preclude you from covering that topic on other content strategy platforms—quite the opposite.

Content can also be graduated, so to speak. The blog post you wrote last week might turn into a newsletter, which might catch the attention of the publisher of an industry magazine who asks you to write an article on the topic for them. When the article gets published and gets significant attention from the readers, maybe that same publication asks you to put together a webinar or talk on the topic for their next conference. This sort of thing happens regularly, in various shapes and forms, but none of it is possible unless you first take the time to write.

ON WRITING WELL

Many intelligent people are panic-stricken over the idea of writing. Writing is an intimate thing, and most of us do not believe that we are very good at it. Practice alleviates many fears, but practice can also entrench bad writing habits that develop over the years.

To help with these issues, I recommend reading William Zinsser's *On Writing Well*. Spend some quality time with this book. The confidence and knowledge you will gain from it will be well worth the ten or so hours you invest reading and thinking about it.

CONTENT STRATEGY PLATFORMS

If you are just beginning your content strategy, newsletters are probably the best way to start. As far as content strategy platforms go, they have it all. Writing a monthly newsletter most likely means that you will add around fifteen hundred to three thousand words of new content to your site each month over the span of two to six web pages (assuming around five hundred words per page). With a newsletter, you have an effective, easy to understand call to action, "Subscribe to Our Monthly Newsletter," and it gets you in front of your prospects each month through the email you send out to them.

These three benefits: the search engine-indexable content, the call to action, and the long-term prospect nurturing, are the primary benefits you aim for from any content strategy platform. Monthly newsletters are also useful because people understand what they are. No one is confused about what signing up to receive an email once a month means. Blogs and webinars are more confusing in terms of the medium through which they are primarily transmitted (RSS for blogs and online web meeting software for webinars). This last point is a subtle one, but if your audience is not particularly tech savvy, it is one worth considering.

Another benefit of the monthly newsletter is that it is a reasonable commitment of time for you to make. You can write two thousand words about what you do once a month, I know you can. Alternatively, a blog has an expectation of frequency to it that can be tough to live up to if you are just starting your content strategy. If the blog (firm-wide, again) has not been updated in more than a few weeks, it can do more harm to your brand than good.

The Email Blast

One important point to bring up here is that the newsletter is more about the content you add to your site than the email blast you send out. Even if you only have two subscribers, your newsletter could play a significant part in your overall marketing effort, so do not allow initial low subscriber numbers to deter you.

Your blast should be carefully considered. Make it focused and brief. The goal of your content strategy is to bring people to your site so that you can wrap them in your experience and further engage them. As an element of your content strategy, the blast is simply a teaser, and its sole purpose is to entice people to come to your site to read your entire newsletter.

The email itself should be branded but also easily understood in plain text format. Include a clear headline that links to the newsletter on your site, a large and engaging image that does the same, a few sentences of summary description, and a link to "read more." In addition, consider having one or two calls to action in the sidebar, but that should be it. Make it clear and concise, and bring people to your site.

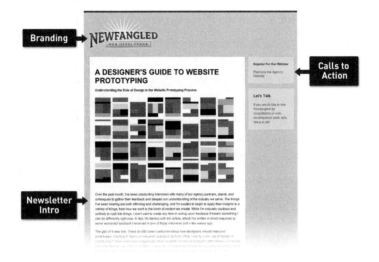

An example of an email newsletter template

I do not believe it matters what type of software you choose. There are many services out there that work fine for this kind of job. I have shopped around a good bit, though, and I do recommend CampaignMonitor.com as an email delivery tool. The pricing model makes perfect sense, it is reliable, and the analytics it provides are top-notch.

One last point to keep in mind about email newsletters is that they provide a great deal of value, even if the recipients do not read them all the time—or even most of the time. Again, the content that goes on your site as a result of the newsletter is visible to search engines and to anyone who visits your site forevermore, and that is an indisputable benefit. However, the email you send out is a subtle reminder to your entire audience that you are still around, you are smart, you exist just to serve them (if you are specialized), and that you are thinking and writing about topics that are relevant to them—possibly even topics which they know their current agency is not knowledgeable about. They can glean all of this in the few seconds it takes them to see your newsletter in their inbox, scan it quickly, and archive it. This brief impression is invaluable, and I encourage you to do all you can to make sure as many of your prospects as possible receive the benefit of this impression.

Blogging

If you are in the habit of creating monthly newsletters and your firm is ready to expand its content strategy, blogging is a natural next step. Blogging makes sense especially for firms that have multiple contributors. If you decide to add a blog to your site, you should commit to adding at least two to four posts to your site each month. Again, if multiple people contribute, this should not be a problem. Some firms map out each month with editorial calendars. This can be a useful tool to keep everyone aware of what is going on around them, and they can compose each post with an understanding of the greater editorial context of the content strategy. Editorial calendars are also a good way to keep people accountable and motivated.

The worst thing that can happen with your corporate blog is for it to go dark a few months after you launch it. There are far too many agency blogs online today that have not been updated in over a month. Do not launch a blog unless you know you can sustain a consistent pace. Some agencies try to get around this by not dating their posts. This only works if no one is paying attention to your blog, and if that is the case, what is the point anyway?

Having a blog is not mandatory. In fact, most agencies cannot commit to creating new and meaningful posts each week and, therefore, should not have a blog. I bring this up because I know that many agencies feel pressure to have a blog, so they start one, and then it peters out. In cases like these, it would be much better to have never started at all.

A good way to test your firm's blogging stamina is to create a blog, but keep it unpublished so that only people inside the firm can see it. If, after three months, you keep up a healthy pace of blogging, you will know that you have a good thing going, and you can release the blog with a significant amount of momentum due to the past three months of articles you're about to release to your audience and Google.

Distributing Your Blog
The way in which people can access your blog is an interesting topic. Blogs were originally intended to be accessed via RSS (Really

Simple Syndication). RSS is a handy piece of technology that allows you to sign up to feeds from the sites you frequent through an RSS reader, such as Google Reader. The idea is that instead of reading a newspaper each morning or going to ten different websites for all the different posts that may interest you, you can instead just go to your RSS reader and let the articles come to you. This makes great sense on paper, and Google Reader is one of Google's most useful applications. However, RSS has not caught on with the mainstream, and if it were going to, I think it would have by now. RSS is still a great vehicle for information delivery and is used by other applications that you might use, but chances are that most of your prospects will not read your blog through an RSS feed.

Does that mean you do not need an RSS feed of your blog? No, it does not. Your blog should definitely have its own RSS feed. The real question is, if people do not access your blog through RSS, how do they access it? If you are lucky, some might be mindful enough to visit your site regularly to keep up with your blog, but I would not count on that.

I suggest adding an email-based call to action for your blog post. Allowing people to receive a weekly, bi-monthly, or monthly summary of your blog in their inbox gives you all the email marketing benefits mentioned in the newsletter section and offers non-RSS users a way of conveniently receiving your content on a regular basis. The frequency of the email depends on how often you blog. Each email should have at least two to three new posts in it.

An example of a blog digest email

It is important to get your message to your prospects through a variety of media so that they can choose how they would like to receive it. While webinars will do little to attract new people to your site since their SEO impact is minimal, they are an effective way to make your firm's expertise more diversely accessible.

Because of the SEO limitation, I do not recommend using webinars as the first element of your content strategy. It makes more sense to start with newsletters or blogs. If you already do one or both of those things, it is not a stretch to repurpose some of that content into webinars.

A good rule of thumb is to plan your webinars to be about thirty minutes in length, followed by up to fifteen minutes for answering any questions from the audience. I find that noon eastern standard time is a good time to broadcast the live webinar. This way, people as far west as Vancouver and as far east as Italy can join at a reasonable hour. Webinars tend to attract a diverse audience, so the time element can be key.

Webinars may seem quite daunting, but there are two tools that make them relatively easy to pull off once you have the material together: GoToWebinar(.com) and Apple's Keynote product.

GoToWebinar is an amazingly feature-rich, affordable, and reliable tool. At the time of this writing, it costs a few hundred dollars per month. With that, you also get unlimited use of their other product, GoToMeeting (which happens to be my web meeting software of choice).

After finding the webinar information on your site, visitors can click on a link and sign up right through the GoToWebinar interface, which is quite simple. After they sign up, you can arrange for them to redirect to a page on your site. GoToWebinar sends out reminders to all registrants a few days before the webinar. For the event itself, it manages the audio, the streaming video from your desktop, a Q&A forum, and chat. Once the webinar is done, it provides you with a report of who attended, who did not, a recording of the presentation, and what the interest level was for each attendee. The tool also lets you customize follow-up emails for both those who attended and those who did not. This is a great way to sneak another call to action in to both parties.

My attendee follow-up email usually goes something like this:

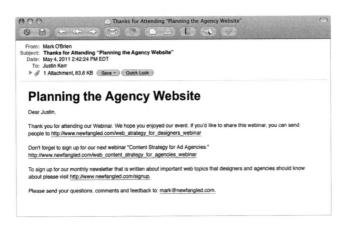

My no-show follow-up email usually follows a similar format but also offers the option to watch the recorded version of the webinar they missed.

This is a great system, and it makes webinars a valuable element of our content strategy. Even if a person does not end up attending the webinar, they have four different impressions of the firm:

1. They found the webinar initially and thought the topic was compelling enough to sign up for it.
2. They received the reminder email a few days prior to the event.
3. They received the no-guilt follow up email that was packed with calls to action.

They are now on your webinar list, so they will hopefully hear from you each time you announce a new webinar.

As far as points of engagement go, this is about as rich as it gets. GoToWebinar can also record the webinar's audio and video. At the end of the presentation, it automatically crunches the webinar into a reasonably-sized WMV file, which we always post to our site within a few hours of the live event. This makes every webinar an effective initial and ongoing conversion point.

The other tool that I believe is essential for webinars is Keynote. I do not know how Apple defeated Microsoft in creating the absolute best office tools (Pages, Numbers, etc.), but they did. Keynote is part of iWork, and its benefits far exceed those of Power Point. Although it takes a little bit of work to gain a full understanding of the program, becoming comfortable with Keynote is worth the time investment for both webinars and public speaking engagements.

MANAGING YOUR FIRM'S CONTENT STRATEGY

Once you have a more complex content strategy, you will probably begin to involve multiple authors throughout the firm across multiple platforms. At that point, it is a good idea to appoint someone on staff as your internal editor. This should be someone who has a solid understanding of the firm's marketing objectives and culture, someone who is organized and adept at educating and motivating people, and, of course, someone with strong verbal and written communication skills. That person may or may not be you. It is an important role that takes a good deal of attention and time. The detail oriented, highly organized skill set required for this role may not fit so well with the general personality profile of the average small agency principal, so be prepared to delegate this exceptionally important role, if need be.

When considering this time and intellectual investment, it helps to view it as a pure marketing cost. How much time and money would you have been willing to spend ten years ago on designing, printing, and shipping three thousand copies of a six-color glossy fold-out brochure? If you invest the same resources into your web marketing (adding more time and less money), you will likely invest enough to see real benefits within six months or so.

The key here is consistency, so I suggest that you start small. Commit, for instance, to writing monthly newsletters, with two thousand words each. Once that becomes a part of your routine, maybe consider starting a company blog. Start with a soft internal launch while you develop the blogging habits as a firm and get a sense of who should and should not contribute and what direction they need. After those two platforms begin to run smoothly, adding quarterly webinars may be a natural next step.

A content strategy that fully embraces any of the platforms I describe here goes a long way toward making your website an invaluable marketing asset. If you cannot take on more than one platform, don't sweat it, but I strongly suggest that you do commit at least to one, and stick with it. </>

/engage/

> How your site can guide your prospects into the next level of their relationship with you

> What calls to action are, why they are so important, and how to craft them

> How to approach on-site social media

> How to nurture your leads

> How to use Google Analytics to keep your site performing well, and how to get more life out of it

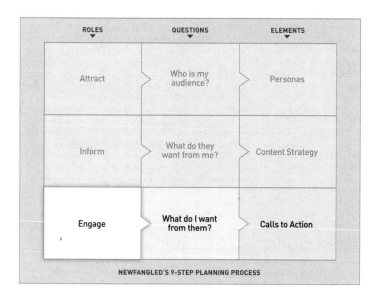

ROLES ▼	QUESTIONS ▼	ELEMENTS ▼
Attract	Who is my audience?	Personas
Inform	What do they want from me?	Content Strategy
Engage	**What do I want from them?**	**Calls to Action**

NEWFANGLED'S 9-STEP PLANNING PROCESS

This last role of engaging your audience is the most important and overlooked of all. All marketing activity should drive the target audience to take action. I understand that this purpose for marketing is not lost on any agencies out there, but it is clear that many agencies do not approach their own sites with this goal in mind.

Once your site attracts the right people and informs and inspires them through your work and expertise, it should then bring those people into some sort of relationship with you. This will not happen by accident; it will only happen if, from the beginning of your planning process, it is your intention.

What do I want from my audience?

It would be great if prospects decided to hire you within a few minutes of first landing on your site, but that is not how these sorts of decisions are made. The modern marketing website is built around attracting prospects who are in the researching stage of the buying cycle, bringing them into your lead-nurturing system, and keeping in close but unobtrusive contact with them until they approach you with an intent to buy.

Because your most potent opportunity lies in attracting prospects in the researching stage, you should acquire two things from them when they first visit your site: their information and their attention.

Both of these things are acquired through your site's calls to action. The prospect who finds your site through a Google search and then identifies it as a valuable educational resource should see a clear, concise, and compelling call to action on the site to receive your content for free on a regular basis. If they land on one of your newsletter pages, for example, they should see a call to action in the righthand sidebar, above the fold, that invites them to sign up to receive your newsletter through email. The ideal transaction is a simple and equitable one: they give you their name and email (and that's about it), and you promise to send them an email every time you add a newsletter to your site—no more, no less.

Once prospects identify your site as an educational resource, they are usually happy to volunteer their names and emails in exchange for the convenience of being notified about your content, as opposed to having to remember to go to your site on a regular basis. If they do not identify your site as a valuable resource, there is not a thing you can do to entice them to sign up for anything—iPad giveaways be damned.

When this transaction occurs, they think (if they even take the time to think about it at all) that the most valuable thing they gave you was their information, but this is wrong. When someone subscribes to receive updates about your content, that person actually gives you a portion of their attention for months—and probably even years—to come.

Getting your prospects' information can be valuable (and in this case, it is better to obtain a few details about many people than many details about a few), but gaining a portion of their attention for the next few years is invaluable. Even if they only read a portion of one out of every ten newsletters you publish, they will be reminded of your firm, your expertise, and that fact that you can answer the questions they have, every time they glance at the newsletters that arrive in their inbox. This regular, subtle, and helpful reminder helps to keep you at the top of their minds when the need to hire a firm like yours arises. If your site succeeds in creating this sort of dynamic among your general prospect base, then it has succeeded as a marketing resource.

Lead Generation

A number of years ago, I read an article that said if the only call to action you have on your website is a link to your "contact us" page, then you have a website without any calls to action. That was one of those simple ideas that had an immediate and memorable effect on me. I realized at the time that my company's website was guilty as charged. We did what so many sites, and agency sites in particular, still do today. We successfully attracted the right people to our site and informed and inspired them through our site content and case studies, but we left it at that, and, therefore, we missed out on the most important part of the process: engaging our visitors.

Within a few weeks of reading that article, Newfangled took drastic action. We added our three calls to action at the time (Subscribe to Our Newsletter, Register for Our Next Webinar, Get in Touch With Us) to the sidebar of every page of our site. That is all we changed. We did not add content; we did not tweak the SEO on the site; we did not drive any new people to our site through new marketing activities. Instead, we simply placed clear calls to action on every page of our site. This one change had a greater effect on our site's lead-generation efficacy than any other single change we have ever made. Before the change, we received, on average, ten or so form signups per week, but afterwards, the signups jumped to an average of fifty to one hundred per week. With such a dramatic response, I finally understood the importance of calls to action.

Only when your site starts generating many high-quality form conversions does it truly begin working for you. At that point, it transforms from a brochure into a real marketing tool.

Let's consider two different site experiences your prospect might have with your site, one with clear calls to action and one without.

Say a potential prospect searches for services like yours one day, and you have been writing newsletters for years on topics in which they are interested. Because of all the valuable content on your site, Google lists you on the first half of the first page for many competitive search terms related to your expertise, and your prospect clicks through one of those listings to your site. So far, so good, but here is where the paths diverge. In scenario A, your site has plenty of useful content, but the calls to action are buried and ineffective. In scenario B, you still have all that content, but each page also has relevant calls to action listed in the sidebar.

Scenario A

A prospect finds your site, reads through a few newsletters, and is inspired and impressed. They know they will be reviewing their agency website in six months, and they make a mental note to remember you and your valuable content at that time.

Unfortunately, after those six months pass, they remember only that they saw a site that had some strong content on it, although they can no longer recall what the articles were specifically about or what the site address was. They even go so far as to go back to Google to search for what they remember of the content that so interested them, but, you never end up hearing from them.

The prospect goes through similar motions. They arrive at your site, read the article Google initially referred them to, and end up reading portions of a few more articles. After the third or fourth page view on your site, they notice a call to action that seems to be speaking to them directly. It reads "Subscribe to Our Free Monthly Newsletter." Beneath that headline is a list of the topics of the past three months' newsletters, each one more interesting to them than the last. Below that is a simple two-field form that asks only for their name and email.

The prospect first began to trust you when Google referred them to your site. After reading one article, they are impressed. After the second or third article, they start to think that this is content they cannot live without (or at least cannot do their jobs as well as they would like to without it). By the time they notice your clear, concise, and compelling calls to action, they are chomping at the bit to sign up.

This is just the beginning. From that point forward, you continually remind them of your expertise through a monthly email. So, at the very least, they think of you once a month. They might click through and read all or some of your articles, and they may skip some, too. Either way is all right. What matters is the impression. Once they sign up for your newsletter, you can personally contact them once a month to remind them that your firm exists specifically to help people like them with their marketing problems. When that agency's review comes up in six months, your firm's name will be at the top of the prospect's mind, and you will have spent the past six months developing an expertise-based relationship with them without ever speaking to them.

Without calls to action, your content strategy is relatively useless. Without a content strategy, your site is a brochure. When both of these plans are in place and working on your site, you have a formidable and tireless marketing machine working for you 24/7.

Calls to Action

Discovering your site's calls to action is easy once you go through the exercises of creating your personas and planning your content strategy. Calls to action are simply points of engagement on your site where your visitors can give you a little bit of their information in exchange for something you are offering. "Subscribe to Our Newsletter," "Register for Our Next Webinar," and "Contact Us" forms are all common calls to action found on marketing websites.

CONVERSIONS: THE ONLY MEANINGFUL FORM OF MEASUREMENT

Often, the agencies I speak with are too focused on site traffic. Unless you are selling ad space on the site you are building, traffic is most likely a poor indicator of true performance. Using traffic numbers to judge the strength of your site, its pages, and the value of the marketing tools you use to drive prospects to the site will quickly lead you to make bad decisions and will make you susceptible to the innumerable SEO/SEM snake oil practitioners out there.

I propose that, instead of traffic, you focus on action—namely, conversions. If a search engine phrase sends one hundred people to your site each month, but they all bounce off the site after reading a single page, well, that phrase is not really having a positive impact on your business. If another phrase sends fifteen people to your site a month, and four end up converting on one of your calls to action, then that is a phrase that deserves attention. The same logic goes for site pages. The ones with the most traffic are not necessarily as valuable as the ones that drive the most site conversions.

CREATING AND MANAGING EFFECTIVE CALLS TO ACTION

So, what makes an effective call to action? Calls to action should follow the three "C" rules: they should be clear, concise, and compelling.

Calls to action need to be clear.

By this, I mean that it should be obvious what it is you are asking of the visitor and what it is they will receive from you. This one is straightforward—think "Subscribe to the Newsletter," "Sign up for Our Weekly Blog Email Digest," and "Register for Our Webinar." Be clear about what you want them to do: "Register," and what it is they will receive: "...for Our Webinar."

Calls to action need to be concise.

For the kind of lead generation most agencies seek to implement on their own sites, it is better to get a small amount of key information about many people than a lot of information about a few people. If a newsletter is the content strategy platform you choose to use for your call to action, you do not need anything more than the subscriber's name (first and last names all in one field, you can auto-split them later), and their email address, as depicted in the image to the right. Getting that prospect's information is valuable, but the real value is that they will be regularly reminded of who you are and how smart you are through your content strategy. The more prospects you can engage in this sort of relationship, the healthier your pipeline will be.

Calls to action need to be compelling.

It is not uncommon to see agency sites that have calls to action asking visitors to "Subscribe to the Newsletter" without any reference to the actual newsletter itself. Sites like that receive few form submissions. Prospects are unwilling to share their information and simply hope for the best. They need to be convinced that the newsletter you write each month is something they need to receive regularly in order to be effective at their jobs. Your content is what will compel them, and it should be thorough and educational, not sparse and promotional.

ON-SITE SOCIAL MEDIA

There is much confusion among marketing firms about how they can best market themselves through social media. If your website is living up to its full potential, it is an educational resource for your clients and prospects. Once your site achieves that status, you will likely start developing a fan base of people who excitedly anticipate your next newsletter, blog post, or webinar.

These fans who you cultivate can be some of your greatest marketing assets, and social media is an excellent way to help them spread the word about you. ShareThis.com and AddThis.com are free and easy to install tools that allow your fans to disseminate your content through their preferred social networks. Chances are good that your prospect's peers may also be prospects for you, so this is a valuable form of sharing.

As an alternative to those free tools, at Newfangled, we use our
own custom designed and programmed sharing widget. Instead
of listing an icon for every social media platform that exists, we
focus on inviting our visitors to email a link for the page they
are on to a friend, share it with Facebook, LinkedIn, or Twitter.
These four choices make the whole sharing idea seem much more
approachable. Since we design it into the page, it also attracts more
attention than the many other sharing widgets that we find to be a
little too ubiquitous and homogenous.This type of custom widget is
not difficult to hand-code. Any developer should be able to build it
to decent design specifications relatively easily.

TWITTER

Since this is a book specifically about planning websites, I will not
say much about offsite social media. I will not tell you how to use
Facebook professionally, for example. However, in terms of your
content strategy, I would be remiss to not mention Twitter.

When Twitter first came onto the social media scene, I thought of
it as analogous to the Happy Days episode in which Fonzi jumped

his motorcycle over a shark: it was the beginning of the end. Twitter seemed juvenile, annoying, and generally not worthy of my time.

As it turns out, I was about as wrong as wrong could be. Today, I think Twitter is the most useful social media tool for marketing firms that have a content strategy. Twitter is an ideal way to broadcast your newly written content and to reach otherwise inaccessible prospects and networks.

If you tweet a link for each new piece of content you create, in addition to tweeting other interesting and non-promotional articles, retweeting relevant content others share, and following and/or thanking everyone who retweets or engages with you on Twitter, you will likely see more and more of your referring site traffic coming from Twitter. Having a retweet link right on your site and having a Twitter sidebar on certain pages that show your recent Twitter activity can also be beneficial.

USER COMMENTING

I intentionally left this topic for the social media section, as opposed to including it in the blog section, because comments are no longer relegated only to blogs. There are many areas of your site where you might want to consider enabling user commenting.

The question is, though, should you allow comments at all? For most sites, there is no wrong answer, but when it comes to the agency website, the answer is yes, you should.

I have mentioned a few times now that one of the jobs of your site is to thoroughly convey the personality and thoughts of the firm. Your site should engender trust with your visiting prospects, and the best way to do that is to give the site as human a touch as possible. One way to do this is by showing your employees' faces on the site and making the pictures big enough for viewers to actually see each person's eyes.

Another way to build trust is to have short and diverse conversations throughout the site. The best way to do that is by allowing comments on key content. Key content might include all of your content strategy elements, although allowing commenting on the portfolio could instigate interesting dialogue, too.

In addition to inviting site visitors to comment on your content, also invite your employees to freely take part in the commenting, both on each other's writings and replying to outside commenters, regardless of if they wrote the original article or not.

Commenting is something you have the opportunity to get comfortable with and develop over time. You are unlikely to be deluged with thousands of comments the moment you allow site commenting—quite the opposite, in fact.

Unlike a forum, which is dead without a profusion of activity, a newsletter with comment functionality but without any comments is not a black eye. This is a good thing, too, because it may take some time before people start commenting on any of your content. Do not despair, though; you are not writing for the sake of the comments.

If you continue to execute a strong content strategy, you will build up a fan base, and fans are likely to comment. The way in which you handle these comments will have a significant effect on the growth of your comment content over time.

When you receive a derogatory comment, delete it. Most commenting tools that you can install or build have notification options. Since you will not be dealing with thousands of comments, I believe it is best to allow comments to be immediately published to the site, instead of being placed into an unpublished review queue. You can set up an email notification that lets the author know anytime someone comments on her post. If anyone makes derogatory comments, she can immediately delete them.

Derogatory means insulting, it does not mean disagreeing. A challenging comment can be a great opportunity because it allows you to convey more of your perspective than was articulated through the original piece of content in question. Always give your fans the benefit of the doubt, assume the best, keep your cool, and be as gracious and edifying as possible.

At Newfangled, we have been writing educational newsletters for over ten years now, and we only started receiving comments a few years ago. Today, it is not uncommon for the comment content on a given newsletter to exceed the word count of the newsletter itself. Comment content is just as attractive to Google as any other content on your site. I view all comments as free content that helps our site visitors get a better sense of who we are as people. To me, that is a win-win.

NURTURING YOUR PROSPECTS

There are so many benefits to committing to a long-term content strategy as an agency. Your own preparations for your articles and presentations will be one of your greatest sources of education over the years. The content you add to your site will serve as a constant advertisement for you, even many years after you write it. But my favorite thing about a well-executed content strategy is the way it nurtures your prospects.

It is a great feeling when you have a tight sales month coming up, and you get a call from a perfectly qualified prospect to whom you have never spoken, and they say something like, "I've been reading your newsletter for years, and I've been waiting for an opportunity to work with you. I think the right project just came across the table." If your site is an educational resource on which your prospects have come to rely, this can happen over time.

When you regularly create content, you have a reason to regularly contact the people who have asked you to keep in touch with them. When a prospect signs up for your monthly newsletter, what they are really saying is, "Please get in touch with me every month to remind me of how adept your firm is at helping people just like me and companies just like mine."

This is how you can nurture leads, and it takes no more effort to nurture one lead than it does ten thousand.

Once you have a site that effectively attracts, informs, and engages, it is important to make sure you manage your leads properly. If you only get ten to twenty leads through your site per month, managing the volume is not an issue. Once you start receiving fifty to one hundred conversions on your call to action forms per month, though, you will probably need a CRM (Customer Relationship Management) tool to keep track of them. If you use FunctionFox or Workamajig, you already have lead management capabilities. If you are not using either of those, I recommend signing up for a basic Salesforce.com account.

Salesforce.com is a useful way to keep track of your leads at a basic level, and it scales as your online marketing sophistication does. If you get to the point where you bring a large number of leads through your site, you can use Salesforce along with a Lead Management

Automation (LMA) tool to do all sorts of fancy marketing operations. For example, you can create an automation process that gathers a list of who signed up for your newsletter and your blog digest and also spent more than sixty seconds on a page on your site about social media marketing. After gathering that list, the LMA tool could then automatically send the list members a promotional email about the social media marketing webinar you have coming up. This is a rather complex example, but you get the idea.

Marketing your firm through a content strategy utilizes all the best parts of marketing. You advertise yourself by truly helping people through your expertise. Done right, you will be smarter, you will win more business, and you can feel pretty good about yourself to boot.

USING ANALYTICS TO UNDERSTAND HOW YOUR SITE IS WORKING

Many businesses do not cherish the idea of rebuilding their website and with good reason. Very few mid-sized companies have a dedicated web person in the marketing department, and the website is just one of many responsibilities a marketing director has. The website is too important to ignore, but they are too busy with all of their other marketing initiatives to pay attention to the site for months on end. This is how it is for agencies, too. Your agency's primary function is not to build and maintain a website for your own firm, but, at the same time, your site is a marketing asset you know you cannot ignore.

This common challenge creates a wasteful web development cycle. The cycle involves spending three to six months every three to five years focusing intensely on the website. After the new site goes live, everyone involved goes back to their real job, and the site recedes back into the shadows. Three to five years later, the site gets so far behind the times that it becomes an embarrassment, and the whole process begins again without anyone really knowing what parts of the old site worked and what did not. Applying ninety-five percent of your investment of time, money, and energy to your website over the course of three months every three years and ignoring the site the rest of the time is not an effective approach to managing your most important marketing asset.

The antidote to this wasteful trend is to spread your effort out over the entirety of your site's lifecycle. Approaching your site in this iterative way starts with paying attention to and becoming comfortable with your site's analytics.

Your website is no longer just an online brochure that you need so that you look like a real business. The website is the marketing firm's most important marketing asset, and to remain competitive, you need to make sure your site works as hard as it possibly can.

When you go through the process of building your site, you make thousands of guesses and assumptions about how your prospects will find your site, navigate through it, and decide to take action from it. No matter how much you prepare, the web development process is replete with guesswork.

When your site goes live, it is not time to forget about it and move on to the next job; it is time to start the long-term process of reviewing its effectiveness on a regular basis and making continuous and subtle changes based on what your site analytics tell you.

GOOGLE ANALYTICS 101

All things considered, Google Analytics is the best web analytics tool on the market. It is free to use and easy to install on your site, so there is no excuse not to have it. Every site you build for yourself or your clients should have Google Analytics installed from the day it goes live.

Once you have it installed, the next crucial step is to log in to it and pay attention to what the data is telling you. That is where things get difficult for some people.

I understand that web analytics data can be intimidating. The average person logs in to their analytics a few times in the three to six months after their site goes live, looks at the basic dashboard data, digs a little deeper, develops a combined sense of apathy and confusion, and never logs in again. The main reason people feel like their analytics are not worth studying is that they do not know what they should look for. Should you care about hits, visitors, bounce rate, time on site, pages per visit, time per page, all of the above, or none of the above? When you do not know what to look for or why, logging in to your analytics account seems like a waste of time.

My goal in this section is not to make you into a certified Google Analytics Consultant, but I do want you to come away from this with an understanding of what you should pay attention to and why your site analytics matter.

THE BASIC DATA: WHAT MATTERS

The main reason people get overwhelmed when they look at their site analytics is that there is just so much information there. What is it all and what does it all mean? Everyone has a sense that paying attention to their site's analytics is important, but the volume of data is so bewildering it feels like you would have to take a course in analytics to be knowledgeable enough to see the forest through the trees. At some point, all the data in Google Analytics has a good reason to be tracked, and you can never really know enough about how to analyze the way your visitors use your site, but here is a run down of the basic elements you can use to keep tabs on how your site is doing.

VISITS

Visit count is the main data point you will view each time you log in, mostly because Google puts that report front and center in the dashboard by default. There are a few things to keep in mind when using visit count to assess how your site is doing.

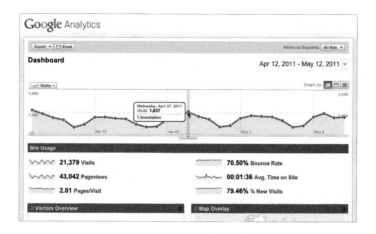

First, visit count and hit count are different. A hit is triggered any time anything is requested from the server. So, if you have a page with thirty images on it, loading that page will trigger at least thirty hits. I never pay attention to hits and neither should you.

Second, while visits can be a good way to track the basic growth of your site, you should not make major site decisions based solely on the goal of simply increasing traffic. The point of your site is not to bring a lot of people in, it is to bring a lot of the right people in and to then get them to do the right things.

In the next section on goals, I will explain how to measure the value of your traffic.

BOUNCE RATE

When a user leaves the site after visiting only one page, that is considered to be a "bounce," and a bounce rate of over forty percent is generally considered to be a problem. People make a big deal about bounce rate, and while bounce rate is an important metric, you need to look deeper than your site's overall bounce rate percentage to get a sense of what is really taking place. When you implement a content strategy on your site, you add a considerable amount of content to your site on a regular basis. This content does not go away; it will slowly build over the years, and before you know it, your site will be hundreds and hundreds of pages deep. If you follow the basic rules of SEO, Google will aggressively index all of those pages, and you will receive a large portion of your traffic from search engines—possibly fifty percent or more.

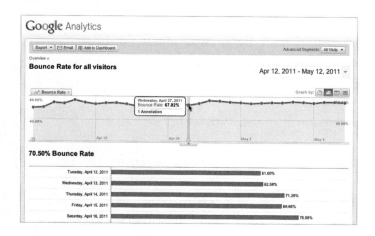

When you begin to have this level of traffic, your bounce rate will undoubtedly increase. Imagine, for example, that you wrote a case study on the packaging design job you did for Pepsi five years ago. A marketing student searches for terms related to Pepsi's marketing history, and Google refers them to that page on your site. Since this student is not interested in hiring an agency, they leave your site after reading that page, and, by doing so, they register as a bounce. Now, you wrote this page quite a while ago, and people do not visit it as often as they used to, and most people who land on this page directly from a Google search might behave in much the same way as that student. Because you have continually added hundreds of pages to your site each year for a number of years, you probably have a number of pages that perform in this way.

Since bounce rate is an average metric that is calculated across every page on your site, your site's overall bounce rate could easily be adversely affected by having fifty or so pages like the one described above. Again, having a bounce rate of over forty percent is generally considered to be poor, but marketing sites for services firms that employ a content strategy tend to have higher bounce rates because of the reality of the situation described above.

Does this mean that you should delete all of those older, higher bounce pages just to reduce your site's overall bounce rate? Hardly. Instead, I encourage you to be cognizant not just of your site's bounce rate, but also of the pages that negatively contribute to it.

If you notice that your site's most crucial pages, such as the home page, portfolio page, and contact page, had bounce rates higher than forty percent, I recommend taking action to remedy the problem. However, if your bounce rate is higher than average due to legacy content on your site, you can let it slide.

PAGES PER VISIT AND AVERAGE TIME ON SITE

These two are the last of the four dashboard metrics I recommend paying attention to regularly. The visits report tells us how many people come to the site, and the bounce rate report tells us how many people leave without investigating further. These two reports give us a sense of session depth in terms of the number of pages people click through per visit and about how long they tend to stay. For a marketing firm site, two to three pages per visit and two or

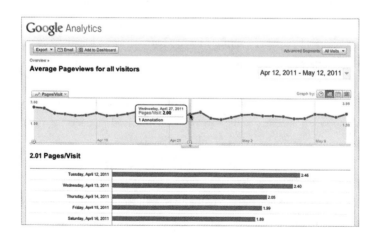

more minutes per session are generally considered to be decent benchmarks. There is no need to pout or cheer if these numbers are off a little on either side, but if there are dramatic trends either way, you may want to investigate the cause.

GOALS

Analytics truly began to make sense to me once Newfangled added goals to our website account. Through goals, you can tell analytics what visitor behavior you are looking for so that you can then see what on your site affects that behavior. For example, you might set "Newsletter Signup" as a goal. You can do so in analytics by assigning to it a name and the URL that indicates when the goal is met. In this case, it is your "Thanks for Subscribing" page. You can create and modify goals from the "Profile Settings" area in your account. I recommend setting up one goal for each call to action you have on your site. Once the goal is in place, Google not only keeps track of how many goals have been completed, but what search engine phrases, referring sites, and site pages led to successful goal conversions.

Goals give context to the way people find and use your site, and they allow you to measure and improve your site based on users' actions, as opposed to doing so based solely on volume of visits.

THREE REPORTS YOU CANNOT IGNORE

Consider that you take the bait and install Google Analytics, and you set up one goal for each call to action on your site. Now what?

Now is the time to pay attention to your analytics and make steady improvements to your site based on your findings. If you spend fifteen focused minutes each week reviewing your analytics from the perspective of the three key reports outlined below and make the appropriate changes in response to the trends you see, you will not only make your site a far more effective marketing tool over the course of its expected lifespan of three years, but you will also likely extend that lifespan by at least another year or so. Set a recurring calendar event for 8:45 every Friday morning, and spend five minutes looking at each of the following reports every week.

Top Content

Found under "Content > Top Content," this report shows what pages on your site are most popular. From the main page, you can dig in a little deeper to get a sense of the navigation trends of your users to and from various pages. The "In-Page Analytics" tool is powerful and offers a clearer idea of how your site is being used than any other single report inside of Google Analytics. Watch out, though, or you will spend all of your fifteen minute allotment just on this.

Referring Sites

Found under "Traffic Sources > Referring Sites," this report shows which other sites send traffic your way. The tabs across the top of this report also indicate which sites contribute to what percentage of goal conversions. If you place ads, trade website links with other companies, or comment on other sites regularly, this report is the way to measure what you earn from your efforts. This report also gives you a good idea of which search engines and social media channels send people your way.

KEYWORDS

Found under "Traffic Sources > Keywords," this report shows you what search engine phrases people use to find your site. Something to pay attention to here are branded versus non-branded keywords. Branded keywords include your company name, and non-branded keywords contain no reference to your name but are usually geared toward your expertise. Since the goal of your SEO efforts is to attract people to your site who do not yet know about you, you should look for a richer mix of non-branded keywords than branded keywords. As your content strategy matures, you will see that this happens naturally. This report also shows you which keywords contributed to what percentage of goal conversions.

THE BENEFITS OF ANALYTICS

With analytics, you can prove or disprove the hypotheses you made when you were building your site. You can also identify and react to market and usability trends that you did not consider when building your site. A weekly review of your site's analytics ensures that you always know the status of your site—what works, what does not, and why. This knowledge allows you to make subtle tweaks and corrections to your site on a frequent basis. These regular site tune-ups can significantly increase the life of your website while making it a continually improving marketing tool.

What's more, you will be much smarter about both web analytics and web marketing in the process. This new knowledge and confidence will be handy throughout the rest of your career as a marketer. Paying attention to your own site's analytics is a win-win: your site will run at maximum efficiency, you will become smarter about web marketing as each week passes, and you can rest easy knowing that you are in touch with the health of your most important marketing asset. </ >

/in_summary/

When you take the time to go through the 9 Step Process I describe in this book, you will have a system for analyzing and planning marketing sites that stand the test of time. When you look at your site, or maybe when you evaluate a client site before a meeting, you will find yourself asking and answering questions like:

> - Is this site effectively attracting, informing, and engaging?
> - Was this site crafted with well-defined personas in mind?
> - Is the site properly optimized for search engines?
> - Are the calls to action present and engaging?
> - Is the site intuitively navigable?

These questions will help you quickly and clearly assess the marketing potential of a website, and you now have the knowledge you need to answer them, regardless of the size and complexity of the site.

I hope this book was a helpful and enjoyable read for you, and I hope it continues to be a reference for you as you approach future web projects. Most importantly, I hope this book helps you more confidently approach web work for your clients and makes you more likely to build your own site into the business-generating tool it ought to be.

Every time I put my thoughts together for a talk, article, blog post, or, in this case, a book, I realize how thankful I am to make my living by helping marketing firms. Whenever I meet a new agency, I am almost always encouraged by how kind, creative, interesting, and intelligent they are. I cannot think of a better group of people with and for whom I have the opportunity to work each day.

If you are interested in digging deeper into some of the topics I touched on in the book, you may be interested in the books and websites listed on the next page. </>

Suggested Resources

WEB DEVELOPMENT TOPICS FOR MARKETING FIRMS

If you have a question about web development, I encourage you to
ask it on the *Newfangled.com* search bar. We have invested many
hours over the years to make the site a true educational resource for
marketing firms. You can sign up to receive our monthly newsletter
at *newfangled.com/signup*.

Positioning and Business Management Consulting for Marketing Firms

David C. Baker's *ReCourses.com*

New Business Development Consulting for Marketing Firms

Blair Enns's *WinWithoutPitching.com*

Persona Development

The User is Always Right by Steve Mulder

Information Design Planning

Communicating Design by Daniel M. Brown
Client vs. Developer Wars by Eric Holter

Content Strategy

Content Strategy for the Web by Kristina Halvorson
The New Rules of Marketing and PR by David Meerman Scott

Usability

<u>Don't Make Me Think</u> by Steve Krug

<u>Rocket Surgery Made Easy</u> by Steve Krug

Jakob Nielsen's *UseIt.com*

Analytics

<u>Web Analytics: An Hour a Day</u> by Avinash Kaushik

<u>Web Analytics 2.0</u> by Avinash Kaushik

SEO

Jill Whalen's *HighRankings.com*

Acknowledgements

Newfangled's agency partners make our day to day lives enjoyable, challenging, and educational. To them we owe everything. Thank you for our livelihoods.

Newfangled's employees allow me to rest easy knowing that I can sell and market Newfangled all day long and that any clients who choose to work with us will receive superb care. Thank you, all, for also affording me the luxury of writing this book and enabling me to look forward to going to work to every day.

Thanks to Chris Butler for telling me when the book was incomplete, for telling me which ten thousand words I should cut, for creating the majority of the images used in the book, and for the thousands of short and long conversations we've had over the years that help keep everything at Newfangled on-course and exciting.

Thank you, Eric Holter, for founding the company in which I found my career. I promise to carry on your tremendous legacy with dignity.

Thanks to David Baker and Blair Enns for the positive impact they have made on Newfangled, our clients, and so many other marketing firms all over the world. Thanks especially to David for publishing this book, for pushing me to write it in the first place, and for all the guidance and help throughout the process.

Thanks also to Eric, Chris, David, and Blair for so heavily influencing my thoughts on the topics dealt with in this book. Your voices are always in my head and have become valuable and integrated parts of my own voice.

My wife, Katy, and our children have opened rooms in my mind and heart that have reframed my life. Their love and support is the starting point for everything else. < / >